I CHOOSE!

I CHOOSE!

Your success is your choice.

PHILIPPE KEREDAN

FOREWORD

I am happy that you can hold this book in your hands today. It is first and foremost the fruit of thousands of hours of coaching (both being coached and having coached). It is also the fruit of many hours of reading and reflection, as well as meetings and conversations I have been lucky enough to have with some exceptional people.

Its purpose is to significantly improve the level of self-confidence of those who will practice the program it contains.

"Self-confidence is the key to success," said Ralph Waldo Emerson. It is a kind of unconscious process that controls our actions and thus influences the results we achieve in our lives.

The practical method presented in this book will teach you how to replace "bad programming" with "good programming".

There are people everywhere experiencing difficulties in life or who have trouble getting up with joy in the morning. They give the impression that they react to, and deal with situations, one after the other, by coping. A bit like a cork floating on the water that changes direction according to the currents and the wind, without any destination of its own.

This is terrible because nothing is inevitable. Our success depends on our state of mind and not on our starting conditions (genetic inheritance, social conditions, etc.). Success is a matter of knowledge; it is enough to simply know how it works and to act accordingly to then be able to get up every morning with enthusiasm even with a challenging schedule.

The opposite is the equivalent to participating in a game without knowing the rules. These rules are the natural laws of success and achievement which we must respect if we want to move forward, but which we are not taught in school, and which parents do not always know.

Let's take two examples, which are not as harmless as they may seem, to get an overview of the state of mind that results from an ignorance of these laws.

When it is time to order at a restaurant, many of us assess the people around us before deciding and ordering our dish. It's mechanical. The guests look to the person in front of them and ask, "And you what are you going to have?" This gives rise to amusing scenes which reveal how our automatisms take precedence over our reason.

It also shows an unconscious need for approval and reassurance, coupled with a chronic inability to make decisions on our own. What is most extraordinary is that some people often allow their decision of what to eat to be swayed by someone else. One might think that this is not a big deal, but it does reveal a certain state of mind. The small, seemingly insignificant things, when added up, determine our attitude and actions, and subsequently produce our results.

If a plane flies from Los Angeles to New York, only a perfect stick position will get it there. A deviation of a hundredth of an inch will remain invisible and will not have any consequences for a long time, but it is in Miami or in the middle of the ocean that he will land. We just need to know where we are, where we want to go, and how to get there.

To know where we are going, we must also determine our goals for ourselves— without being influenced by anyone nor anything, — and consider only what we really want.

In a second example, when we ask a person currently earning \$5,000 a month what he would like to earn, a typical answer is \$5,500 or \$6,000. This is absurd! That's not what he wants at all; he wants ten times as much. His answer is self-censorship. The man didn't say what he *wanted,* he said what he *thought was possible for him to get,* and that difference is crucial.

We must aim for and achieve what we really want and refuse to settle for what we now believe we can achieve.

The saddest part is that he probably won't succeed, because it is very difficult to motivate oneself or to maintain a desire starting from a bland objective. There is no deep emotional impact. Like a mother who manages to lift a car because her child's leg is stuck underneath. Would she have managed to get her neighbor's vanity case back?

We must understand that our countless unconscious and deep-seated beliefs, such as those of this man, are holding us all back. Lack of faith in our ability to achieve our goals is the main cause of our failures.

At the same time, millions of people are happy and create their own destiny because they know the right mechanisms.

For you to obtain the best results, I have written the second part of this book in the form of a program in order to accompany you during its reading and to suggest actions to be undertaken to obtain quick effects. These conditions are like coaching sessions.

Too often I have seen people devour one self-help book after another without their lives changing one iota.

The accumulation of information produces no results if it is not accompanied by know-how. Former students who do not have a fully satisfying job will understand.

What we want are positive, quick, and concrete results. All we are interested in is that our lives improve; the rest is just literature.

In this second part, you will take on the lead role, becoming at the same time writer, director, and main actor of your life. Your life will become the realization of your desires rather than the consequence of hazard and circumstances.

On this subject, for those who would be tempted to skim over this second part or to do the program later, I nevertheless invite you to read very closely chapters 15 and 18, which are undoubtedly the most important in this book.

We must freely choose, without any limitation, our dwelling, our achievements, our habits, our profession, our sources of income, our occupations, and our possessions. It's all about methodology and self-confidence. The only rule is to consistently demand the highest quality of all these elements.

I am putting in your hands a real *recipe for success* considering the many *desirable* effects I have seen around me in the people I help. Evolution is necessary for humans. A whole chapter is devoted to this point in this book.

Some ideas will be developed several times from different angles. The conclusion will be the same, but this form of repetition is essential to impact a brain that has adopted many of its current, negative beliefs in the same way; through incessant repetition, for years.

I invite you to welcome this process with a new spirit and to forget your current logic. As Einstein said, it is impossible to achieve better results with the current way of thinking.

Very often, we get bad results but believe ourselves to be doing well, either due to a lack of knowledge, or because we don't take the appropriate actions that would bring us true success.

People who find themselves caught in quicksand usually start to walk out of it as if they were on a staircase. This may seem logical; however, this attitude will prove fatal. They are unaware that they must lie down and move as little as possible to find salvation. Many of the mechanisms of success are the same; they are counterintuitive.

Finally, I also invite you not to read this book too quickly because it is an initiation for the subconscious that needs to have time to record information. It would also be a good idea to keep a stabilo or a pen within reach. by reading more than one chapter a day in the image of a novel it is certain that you will deprive yourself of many benefits.

In truth, it is as much about studying as reading, and in doing so you will see that the subject of study is not the book, but yourself

I wish you a good reading and assure you of my confidence in you to achieve your goals. I do not doubt for a moment that you will succeed.

Part One
The Concepts

Part One

The Computer

CHAPTER 1
SELF-IMAGE

"If I have lost confidence in myself, I have the universe against me"
Ralph Waldo Emerson

When I was a kid, I loved watching old movies. I especially liked the cloak and dagger ones in which the swirling Errol Flynn raged. He was the hero of the action movies of Hollywood's golden era.

To describe this character in a few words, I would say that at the age of thirty, he was, on the screen as in life, the ultimate archetype. He had it all. He was handsome, tall, athletic, friendly, and had a permanent smile. He practiced all sports: tennis, rowing, boxing, skiing, swimming. He flew his planes and navigated his boats himself and had lived a thousand lives. Before making films, he had worked in all sorts of unusual and obscure jobs and had traveled all over the world, on many continents and in the South Seas; he was a true adventurer. When he became an actor, he was instantly one of Hollywood's biggest stars and certainly the most flamboyant. Everyone at the time wanted to meet him and be among his friends. He was an art-lover— he owned paintings by Gauguin and Van Gogh— and wrote books.

Twenty years later, Errol, ruined, bowed out lamentably at only fifty years of age. He died of a heart attack in Vancouver in a small hotel room, and the doctor who performed the autopsy declared that he had discovered the battered body of an old man. The photos of our hero's final years show an unhappy, disfigured man who is not even a shadow of what he was even ten years earlier.

In fact, throughout his life, he partied more than he should have, and this Apollo had destroyed himself through all kinds of abuse.

I only learned all this a little later, of course, in my early teens, and it was a huge shock to me. How could such a character have managed his existence in this way, moving towards such a tragic destiny? In everyone's opinion, this man was perfectly intelligent, so how on Earth could he have run his life so stupidly?

More generally, how is it that we almost always know what actions to take to improve our lives, and that we don't do them systematically; far from it? Why then do we sometimes entertain harmful thoughts without immediately rejecting them? Why do we commit acts that negatively impact our existence?

No doubt, I became aware in that moment that our steps are guided in a sure and certain way by something other than our intelligence and our brain. That it is not the conscious part of the latter that manages our behavior and the way we act, but the unconscious part; this was a revelation for me.

We humans are not *rational* beings, but *emotional* beings, and we will see later that the emotional part of our brain is in direct relation with our unconscious; where our habits are set.

So, it is our emotions that drive us, not our reason. This explains many things and helps us to understand why we sometimes do certain things despite all logic. It also explains wars, crimes, addictions, and many other absurdities.

The quality of our lives depends more on the habits we have created than on our choices. Our habits create our destiny. For example, when we intentionally decide to reach for a cup, the movement of our arm is actually modulated by deeper elements that we may not be aware of— only those who have never spilled a drop of tea or coffee in their lives may want to contradict me. Another example: when we meet someone, we greet them, and we say hello. This is a conscious action, but, by and large, it is our unconscious mind that has handled our attitude, the way we reach out, the strength of our grip, the expression on our face, our smile, and a whole bunch of other things that we can't keep under control twenty-four hours a day.

So, we choose our actions carefully, but we do not fully control how they are carried out, since much deeper mechanisms are involved.

This "thing" that keeps control is the *self-image*. It is the sum of our deep beliefs about ourselves. It determines our level of confidence, our results, and guides our life. Every human being has one, without exception.

When we change our image of ourselves, we automatically change our perception of the world and what surrounds us— a bit like the principle of communicating vessels. All studies and scientific research have come to the same conclusion: among the main causes of success or failure is the profound image we have of ourselves. Horace said, "He who has confidence in himself leads men".

When we talk about success, we are, of course, talking about success in the broadest sense of the word. Social success is only one element. One good definition of success is Earl Nightingale's definition: the progressive realization of a worthy ideal.

This deep image begins to form right after we are born and changes throughout our lives. Our mind is marked by all the events that we perceive with five of our nine senses: what we see, hear, feel, smell, or taste impacts our memory. This information is classified in our unconscious mind to form a program, and the very first years of our life are decisive. At this young age, there is no selection or filtering possible in a being who has not yet acquired the ability to reason.

All information given to a young child is considered by him to be true. When we tell him that Santa Claus exists, he necessarily believes us. His memory is still blank, and no experience is recorded. If we light a lighter in front of him, he will try to touch the flame.

As this child grows older, one day he begins to think for himself but by that time, many beliefs are already registered in his brain. This is not a problem if he revises the beliefs as he grows, but this is not always the case.

If you give to a child a cake for the first time and he finds it tastes good, he will naturally conclude that he likes cake. If, when he tastes other pastries, he finds them excellent too, this belief that he likes cakes or sugar will be reinforced. As he grows older, he will develop this taste. Since it is natural to repeat the pleasurable actions, he will consume more and more pastries. Gradually, he will be led to think that he is greedy (self-image), especially if this remark is also often repeated to him by others. Caught in a spiral, he will then behave according to this belief and devote himself with enthusiasm to the pleasures of the table. This sequence may one day have an impact on his figure as well as on his health.

This person's life could be totally different in this area if the first cakes he was offered had displeased him. This illustrates the importance and randomness of events on one's fate and character formation.

In Asia, mahouts tie young elephants to a tree with a chain that they will wear all their life. As adults, the elephants could easily break the chain and leave, but it doesn't even occur to them. They "know" that the chain is too strong. They tried a thousand times to break it, in vain, when they were small.

Dog trainers are also familiar with the phenomenon, as it plays a role in the height of the fences behind which they keep their puppies. As adults, these dogs may be able to climb over them, but their certainty that they can't will prevent them from even trying. Their brains have definitively closed the file.

Without an emotionally powerful event, such as an earthquake or a fire, these animals will remain trapped in their chains and mental barriers. We humans often function in a similar way, closing our mental files irreversibly. Our profound beliefs are only subjective points of view or "truths" that we have formed, in part, during childhood and before we can even think. They do, however, determine our behaviors throughout our existence.

Ideas can also be passed on from one person to another: let's imagine that during a polo game in his youth, our grandfather had a very bad fall when he fell off his horse. This left a deep impression on him and he repeated this idea to us each time we were both in the presence of a horse. We may then have developed a *preconceived notion* about horses, thinking that these animals are dangerous, that we don't like them very much, and that we are afraid of them.

Thus, these identical phenomena came to repeat themselves in the same way in other fields, leading us to develop different fears. We are likely to end up thinking that we are fearful (self-image) and adapting our behavior accordingly. This is also how others will perceive us.

Personal, negative conclusions drawn from our first experiences— or those of others— can become barriers that prevent us from evolving. Long after we have forgotten the experiences that fed our conclusions, they are still present and active in our minds. This illusory portrait of ourselves continues to form according to our thoughts and perceptions, as events unfold.

In addition, we are besieged with information from all of our senses, but also from our parents, our school, and our friends first, and then from the media: internet, television, newspapers, reading, etc.

Let's take another example: if a young child asks someone for something and that person gives it to them, chances are, the child thinks that you get things by taking action and asking for what you want. When he wants something else, he will ask for it again, which will lead him to become enterprising and voluntary.

If, on the contrary, the thing he asked for has been refused and he has even been scolded for asking for it, if this situation repeats itself a certain number of times, he will probably not ask for anything more. This is in order to avoid any new unpleasant experience. He will also think it is useless to be voluntary or enterprising. He will become shy and self-effacing, and his image will suffer; not to mention his life.

As incredible as it may seem, the same child will have become an assured or self-effacing adult depending on the circumstances, without this having anything to do with what constitutes his deepest being. The quality of education is therefore decisive. Authoritarian parents will transmit their frustrations to their children who will not be able to develop freely. Children brought up by evolved parents will be educated and guided in their progression according to their own tastes and desires.

Generally speaking, a child who is encouraged and complimented by his parents will be confident and balanced and will have a much better chance of succeeding in life than a child who is constantly demeaned and raised in a critical manner.

This self-image continues to change throughout life, but there is a field where it is easily destabilized and questioned. It is that of romantic relationships due to their high emotional content. It can take only a little to have a profound impact. Even as an adult, being confronted on the street with a person of the opposite sex who looks away, refusing to respond to a smile, can have real consequences.

However, since this deep self-image is always in motion, we are now going to be able to work on it in order to modify it. We are going to review the parts that warrant reviewing and validate those that we consider favorable.

Key points of the chapter:

- ☑ We all have an image of ourselves, a self-image that is deep and not conscious.
- ☑ It is created according to our subjective thoughts and emotions, in contact with events.
- ☑ It therefore depends mainly on hazard and circumstances.
- ☑ We are emotional beings, not rational beings.
- ☑ This is why our emotions take precedence over our logic and reason.
- ☑ Self-confidence comes directly from this self-image.
- ☑ The quality of our lives depends directly on the quality of this image.
- ☑ We can change this image at any time, and we will not hesitate to do so.

CHAPTER 2
INDEPENDENCE

"Be yourself, others are already taken"
Oscar Wilde

We have seen in the first chapter how we form some of our beliefs and our profound image.

Sometimes we do things that are so absurd that it is better to laugh than to cry, as the saying goes.

While watching his mother prepare a leg of lamb, a young boy notices that she cuts off the end of the bone and throws it in the garbage before putting the dish in the oven. He asks her why she is doing this, as it seems unnecessary. His mother replies that this is how a leg of lamb is cooked and that she has always done it this way. The boy insists and she ends up answering that she learned it from her own mother, and that, the next time he sees her, he will just have to ask her why a leg of lamb is cooked like that.

When he can do so, his grandmother tells him that when she was young, she was extremely poor and since her oven was very small, she had to cut the bone so that the leg would fit in it. She had continued to do this afterwards out of habit.

This is the phenomenon of mimicry, which we can adopt our whole life, not only for attitudes, but also for some of "our" ideas. In fact, we model countless behaviors on those of others, and then our reason takes over to justify these acts, finding explanations for them that have nothing to do with reality, and allowing us to believe in our autonomy. All this is obviously totally unconscious.

When we suggest to a person under hypnosis that they are thirsty, they start drinking when they are woken up. If we ask why they drink, they will justify it by saying that it is hot or that they haven't drunk for a long time. But this is not the real reason. If they began drinking, it's because it was suggested to them. Every day we do this without realizing it because that's the way we operate. Therefore, we have every interest in becoming more aware, through knowledge, in order to become more autonomous.

Some might say that it doesn't matter, that it's not useful to think about these things, but this is a mistake. By not freeing ourselves, we limit our potential much more than we can imagine. Moreover, we are here to achieve *our* goals, not those of others. As Oscar Wilde humorously said, we are here to live our own lives, not the lives of others.

This implies having personal values that correspond to our way of thinking, rather than conforming to those of others. For each of our beliefs, the result can be beneficial or negative for us, and our unconscious mind records the information and impacts us accordingly. If an identical fact occurs again, the force of repetition will have the effect of imprinting our personal program more deeply. The stronger the sensation or emotion, the deeper and more lasting its influence will be on the image we form.

These last two elements— the *strength of emotion* and *repetition*— are essential, as they will soon serve us to modify our deep image.

Some of our beliefs have been deeply rooted in us through incessant repetition over the years, and we will have to lay siege to our unconscious on all sides at once, yet again for our actions to be effective. This time, however, we will act consciously, considering only our desires and what we really want.

We are all basically the same, for the simple reason that we all belong to humans. Only our actions and results differ, and these depend on our points of view which are only subjective truths. Anyone who thinks that they are different or inferior in any way from his fellow human beings is mistaken because confidence is not a genetic element.

Being truly oneself implies building a strong self-image, but also being less dependent on others, on the vagaries of life, and on external circumstances.

However, a strong self-image should not be confused with an oversized ego— a phenomenon that we sometimes encounter in people and which we will present now; the two are diametrically opposed.

He who displays too strong an ego is a bragger; his ego constitutes an appearance, a bit like a Superman costume that one puts on to appear superior, or like Jean de La Fontaine's frog facing the ox. The ego also manifests itself in what some people call a superiority complex, whose role is precisely to mask a feeling of inferiority or insecurity. A person with an oversized ego is therefore the exact opposite of a truly secure person.

To use an allegory, this kind of ego is like a "tuned" car with a stainless-steel exhaust system that bounces back and forth at red lights. The strong self-image, in comparison, would be a Ferrari that starts off quietly, slowly, and without worrying about its position.

Lao-Tseu summarized this concept as follows: "He who knows, does not speak. He who speaks, does not know".

Boasting, intransigence, anger, and all forms of show-of-force are always suspect. It is better to consider them as an admission of weakness or an evidence of fragility. In the face of such demonstrations, let us feel compassion for the person, rather than let ourselves be impressed.

Successful people are regularly misrepresented as having too strong an ego when in fact they have a strong *self-image* which is very different. They are creators, not competitors, except during an event. They are not interested in power relations because they have nothing to prove. They are advancing for themselves and to *help* others, not to *impress* them. A strong self-image is the expression of real power. It is dynamic but peaceful and benevolent.

It seems better to compete with oneself than with others.

Refusal to evolve also often represents a demonstration of pride since to evolve is to admit that what we are or what we do can be improved. The ego transforms change into self-criticism, which is then experienced as a personal aggression and an attack on one's own value.

This is what lies behind convictions and habits. As Nietzsche said, "The enemy of truth is not lies, but convictions".

It is both subtle and unconscious, but it is inappropriate pride that prevents people from evolving. This attitude is reminiscent of the child who crosses his arms and stomps his foot, saying no firmly, and staying in his position.

There is a story about this: a teacher asks his students, "Who wants change?" All the students raise their hands. The second question he asks them is, "Who wants to change?" There are no hands raised anymore.

Having a life in which the days follow one another, and each look alike is a trap. However, it is easy to avoid once you become aware of it. A bit like subliminal images hidden in a film or a report to influence us. As long as we don't know they are there, they have a powerful effect on us, but once we know they are there, they lose all effectiveness as tests on the subject have shown.

Let's be sure that as we progress in reading this book— and especially as we begin to work concretely in the second part— our ego will do everything it can to play tricks on us and to try to slow us down, in order to ensure its survival.

This will come in the form of limiting thoughts; we will tell ourselves that we don't have time to work, or that it's not necessary, etc. These thoughts will have no other purpose than to dissuade us from acting. We will ignore them while moving forward. The ego defense mechanism will seek to bring us back to our old patterns of thought and action. Our old image— the one that has guided us until now— will not want to disappear in favor of the new, more efficient one that we will gradually replace it with.

Coming back to some of our actions, we sometimes give into ease or laziness in order to avoid thinking, and then we fall back into our habits and our conditioning.

How many times do we complicate our lives by, for example, driving down a longer or more congested road in order to avoid the effort of studying a better route before leaving? In our life, it is the same: if we took the time to think a little more, we could better adapt our itinerary and we could reach our destination more quickly.

In some traditions or in the case of the lamb bone, this is not a big deal. When we develop a fear of horses or animals, as in the previous chapter, it is already more embarrassing. And if it leads us to adopt addictive and destructive behaviors like dear Errol Flynn, it is dramatic.

Self-destruction is not always physical. It can also be mental, and always manifests itself in the same way; self-sabotage which halts progress.

Some adults remain, as we have seen, at the stage where a lot of childhood misinformation is held as truth and has never been questioned all their lives.

This phenomenon takes full effect in front of a person who represents some form of authority. Faced with the information transmitted by the media, for example, the process is the same: some people accept everything they hear and repeat it without blushing during their conversations, and without any personal analysis or reflection. It makes you wonder if they are not living in a state of hypnosis, under the control of a flat screen or those around them!

This is where we find our attitude as children towards our parents. Common sense is inoperative. Information penetrates directly into our unconscious, without any filter. In this case, we free ourselves from our brain in favor of a "sponge," and it is here that we function with a self-image that was built up during our childhood.

All this should allow us to not judge ourselves too harshly. For my part, without any religious considerations of course, I think that the great phrase, "Let he who has never sinned cast the first stone," is applicable in many circumstances. This is especially true since our way of judging others can also be questionable as we will see later when we talk about projections.

Thankfully not everything is all black or all white, and these elements make things complex. One can have a positive self-image in one area and a negative one in another. Many people are successful in some areas and totally lost in others. You can be an Olympic gold medalist and still have a terrible family life and no friends. You can be the head of a very successful business and still have poor health due to poor nutrition. You can be a global star and feel lonely and very unhappy. There is no shortage of examples and combinations.

This is also true for the people we choose to be around— consciously or unconsciously— for better or for worse.

A gentle woman may find herself with a despotic husband who makes her go through hell, or a brave man may marry a cantankerous woman who turns his life into a succession of reproaches and mood swings. It is one thing for opposites to attract, but only if the resulting combination allows the two elements of the couple to mutually improve their lives. Otherwise, their choice is akin to masochism.

Both above may be the result of poor self-image, or they may be the result of reenactments of family scenarios, as in the case of the lamb bone.

At the beginning of our lives, our parents are our only role models. They are the norm and naturally, we often choose to imitate them. In the case of the son, crushed throughout his youth by a tyrannical mother, he will later choose a "copy-pasted" wife who will make him live the same thing, reproducing a pattern he knows all too well. Or that of the daughter with a dictatorial father, who will also reproduce this model with an identical husband. Unfortunately, these cases are common.

Fortunately, these distressing situations are simply related to a personal misuse of the unconscious, which is neutral, as we will see in a future chapter.

We always come back to the impact of circumstances on our destiny.

Today, science is beginning to understand that cellular degeneration is due less to poor cell quality than it is to unhealthy habits, negative thoughts and stress. The causes of disease are thought to be more psychological than physical.

Genetics is then relegated to the background. We now speak of epigenetics. The acquired takes precedence over the innate, and the quotation that best sums up this approach is that of behavioral specialist Karl Menninger: "Environment is more important than heredity". However, if people get sick for mental, not physical reasons, it is not a conscious choice.

This chapter has allowed us to clarify what the self-image is, and it should, above all, not incite us to pessimism. All "being" in the head, it becomes obvious that it takes no more energy to form a good self-image than it takes to form a bad one.

No matter where we are, we can all make great progress. It's just a matter of method and knowledge.

Key points of the chapter:

☑ We all basically have the same brain and the same mind.

☑ The conception of our deep image can go back to childhood.

☑ Whatever the result, 99% of our parents thought they were doing the right thing consciously.

☑ We can adopt the beliefs of others without realizing it.

☑ Demonstrations of strength are often synonymous with an admission of weakness.

☑ Intransigence and refusal to change are a manifestation of pride.

☑ No matter where we are today, we can all make tremendous progress.

CHAPTER 3
THE UNCONSCIOUS AND HOW IT WORKS

"The growth of the personality is done from the unconscious".

C. G. Jung

Our *self-image* monitors and regulates the quality of our lives without ever lowering its guard. Its mode of operation is quite easy to understand, and we can compare it to three instruments: a thermostat, a GPS, or the autopilot of an airplane.

Like the latter, it keeps control and steers us to our destination in a safe and certain way. Even when we deviate or take another path, it picks us up where we are to take us inexorably back to our destiny.

Therefore, good resolutions do not stand the test of time because we are under the control of our *paradigm, which is the sum of our habits,* without ever resting.

It is also for this reason that it is impossible to change a person's behavior in the long term with the help of simple recommendations or instructions (I am referring here to a professional or educational context, as it is pathological to wish to change others outside of such settings).

To improve our lives or change our results, we need to work in depth. It is not a matter of will. In fact, the latter, just like the efforts made, is in the conscious part of our brain. It is on the unconscious part of the brain that we must focus our attention.

This is also why some people lose and then regain a total of "tons" over a lifetime of dieting. One simple decision and effort are not enough over time. If these people had changed their self-image by revising their way of functioning in the face of this challenge, they would never have had to go on a diet, or at least the first one would have sufficed.

For the same reason, some people eat large quantities of food from morning to night without ever gaining weight, while others gain weight just at the sight of food. The explanation is not genetics, but the way the body regulates food under the control of the brain.

All this shows us again that there are unconscious mechanisms of control and, when necessary, progress must be made gradually. There is a risk of failure involved in rushing through the stages, which is why working on oneself must remain gradual.

Let's take the results achieved by salespeople, shopkeepers, restaurateurs, artists, and sportspeople, to name but a few. From one year to the next, year-end balance sheets follow one another and look the same unless there is a real internal change.

As far as salespeople and sales representatives are concerned, a significant difference (ten times is not unusual) in performance can be seen between two people who they offer the same product. However, each of them will obtain the same individual results from year to year.

If one of these salespeople "goes off the road" with an exceptional sale, their internal GPS will take them back to their destination— their usual annual result— reducing their subsequent performance. Every business leader knows this.

If an unaccustomed soccer player scores three goals in a game, there is a good chance that he will lift his foot off the gas and close out the month's goal rate at his usual level of performance. If, on the other hand, he is seen to be as effective in one game after another, it will mean that a profound change has taken place in him.

This phenomenon is the same for children at school and for everyone in their relationships; always, a kind of pattern is reproduced.

We must admit that this often looks like a model. It is the "paradigm" already mentioned above. This observation is valid in all fields. It is the cause that needs to be addressed, not the consequences, and this cause lies in the unconscious part of our brain.

In this book it is not necessary to worry about making a distinction between the unconscious and the subconscious. To get better results in our lives— which is the purpose here— it is enough to use the word "unconscious" as being the not conscious part of us.

For the same reason we will not deal here with collective memories and traumas we may have inherited from our ancestors.

The discovery of the unconscious is attributed to Freud who identified and analyzed it during experiments on subjects under hypnosis. He saw that by being placed in this state, some of his patients remembered facts that they were not aware of in the waking state. They were also carrying out some of his instructions without knowing why, since they had been given them under hypnosis.

This does not detract from Freud's genius, but it is obvious that many human beings have been "conscious of the unconscious," if I may say so, since the dawn of time. Socrates', "know thyself," of course alludes to the depth and complexity of the human soul.

Exactly at the same time, 2,500 years ago, Agathocles of Syracuse, King of Sicily, decided to invade North Africa. On several ships, he and his troops sailed across the Mediterranean to land on the side of present-day Tunisia. Once there, he ordered his soldiers to burn all his ships. His men now had only one option: advance and defeat— which they did— as there was no turning back.

The way Agathocles motivated his troops shows that he, too, understood the subtle workings of the brain and its unconscious mechanisms. This is where the expression, "having nothing to lose," takes on its meaning. In this situation, one usually sees oneself sprouting wings and acting.

Later, Nietzsche would say, long before Freud, "If thoughts come to me when they want and not when I want, is there not a psychic phenomenon that escapes consciousness?"

Let's now look at the unconscious in a simple way; we'll just deal with what we need to know in the framework we're dealing with. This fascinating and still mysterious theme is the subject of many books.

The unconscious records our sensations, feelings, and emotions. Let's consider it as the emotional part of our brain. It therefore reacts to pleasure and not to logic.

The unconscious is the realm of *causes*, while the conscious is that of *consequences*.

The unconscious perceives, classifies, and records tirelessly, any thought transmitted to the consciousness by the imagination or by one of the senses. It is active twenty-four hours a day, operates or expresses itself day and night in the form of dreams, slip-ups, missed acts, actions, or reactions, and keeps control.

It is permanently bombarded from all sides and it expresses itself in all the sensations it prints.

It is in the unconscious that all our habits are set.

The unconscious cannot tell the difference between reality and imagination. It is thanks to this primordial fact that we can reprogram it quickly. If we imagine an event in a certain way— as we will learn to do— the result will be the same as if we had experienced it.

The unconscious does not select and cannot reject any information it receives; its database has unlimited storage capacity and memory.

Our beliefs are not the only ones that are controlled by our unconscious. The same is often true of our reactions, whether physical or mental; redness, sweating, trembling, or tension are examples.

The unconscious only recognizes the subject of the theme addressed, without nuance or distinction; it does not differentiate between a negative sentence and a positive sentence. Whether you say, "I am sick," or, "I am not sick," it is received the same way by the subconscious. It only perceives the word, "sick," and it is on this word that it focuses.

It is therefore essential to think and speak with this in mind: if we want to be healthy, let's arrange ourselves to think, "I am healthy". Let's never say, "I'm never sick".

So, if you want to drink less alcohol, for example, it's better to imagine drinking water often rather than thinking about drinking wine less. A person who has debts will think about prosperity rather than settling their debts.

Here's a fun exercise that Dr. Murphy taught us in one of his books: Can you convince yourself *not* to think of a green hippopotamus? Try it. You'll see. If you think, "I shouldn't think about a green hippopotamus," what do you have in mind? A green hippopotamus!

As we can see, the functioning of our unconscious is very different from that of our conscious reality.

The unconscious also allows us to feel unhappy while sipping a cocktail on a heavenly beach or, on the other hand, to feel good with a happy thought in dark circumstances. It knows only our present mental state.

It is neutral. It is not an evil tool created to hinder us, on the contrary. When we understand how it works, it will be of great help to us in the fulfillment of our desires. The unconscious waits to know our projects before helping us realize them, and without worrying about moral values.

Ideas are implanted by feeling. No idea can be implanted in the subconscious if it is not *felt*. This is good news, because if we have negative thoughts, we can immediately reject them.

We can reject any information coming from outside in the same way. If someone gives us bad news, we can simply reject it before we get emotional about it.

We can conceive of the unconscious as a car whose consciousness is the driver. A car is a great tool to take us to our destination, provided the driver performs the right maneuvers. If he stops controlling his vehicle, or if he controls it badly, he will have an accident.

It can also be compared to the memory of a computer. It would then be the part that manages and maintains control of the machine's operation and the conscious part would be the computer screen.

It is in this way that the unconscious must be understood.

Key points of the chapter:

- ☑ Our self-image guides us irremediably and relentlessly like a GPS.
- ☑ For a change to be lasting, it must be profound.
- ☑ The essential element is the unconscious cause, not the conscious consequence.
- ☑ The unconscious can only help us realize our goals if we solicit it in the right way.
- ☑ It makes no difference between an imagined event and a lived event.

CHAPTER 4
THE RESULTS

"That the strategy is beautiful is a fact, but don't forget to look at the result"

Winston Churchill

As it is not conscious and deep, it is not easy to objectively define the image we have of ourselves. Nevertheless, we have an excellent lead for this. This track consists of looking with lucidity and hindsight at the different aspects of our existence, which are our *results*.

These are the outer expressions of our inner image. Let me study your results, and rest assured that I will get a good idea of your deep image because they never lie.

In general, are you happy? Healthy? Do you have many friends? Are you among the best in your field? Do you travel according to your desires? Etc.

Now let's look at the different aspects of our lives in a very precise and detailed way. Here are a few examples of questions to help us discern our results:

- Am I happy?
- What do I look like?
- Am I in good physical condition?
- What are the states of my family relationships?
- Are my children flourished?
- Do I have many friends?
- Do people come to me naturally, or do I go to them?
- Do I spend my time watching television?
- How are the people I hang with?
- Do I like to undertake or create?
- Is my schedule busy ?
- What are my professional results?

  - I work in sales: what are my numbers? How many products or contracts have I sold? Am I performing well ?
  - I am a doctor: do my patients heal quickly?
  - I am a singer: how many albums have I sold? How many people attend my concerts? How many followers do I have on Instagram, Facebook, and YouTube?
  - I'm the center forward of my soccer team: how many goals do I score per month?

That's what results are all about; both our behavior and the fruits we reap.

In this first round of questions about our results, I deliberately avoided talking about money, because in some countries the subject remains somewhat taboo. It seems to me, however, that now is the time to dwell on it a little.

Above all, it is essential to never forget that money itself today has no intrinsic value. The time when we traded in food and gold is over thanks to a very benevolent financial sleight of hand, we know find ourselves with bits of paper and lines on a computer screen instead of gold. We'll see where it takes us to have tolerated that.

Understanding the notion of "value" is necessary now more than ever. There is no question that money is not the supreme value. Of course, love and health, among other things, bring forth nobler feelings, but it so happens that we have created a society in which money provides knowledge, travel, entertainment, comfort, and every conceivable object.

Why wouldn't we be entitled to it?

It is not shameful to lack wealth, of course, but neither is it honorable to deprive oneself of it or to want to deprive one's neighbor of it.

In any case, it's better to defy the *love* of money, rather than money itself. Besides, experience has shown us that it very often reveals or amplifies people's character, in both good and bad ways instead of changing it.

Money is also a crucial gauge to evaluate our *self-image*, but this element should not frighten us.

Many people who were *previously* disadvantaged and without qualifications have gone from being unemployed to being successful entrepreneurs in a matter of weeks. Due to the speed of change in the world and opportunities today, this evolution will soon be possible in just a few hours...

The limit is inside us, not outside. The first step to success is to pay no attention to our current results or external circumstances, and to remain focused and active towards our goals.

Money is a fluid and opulence, and it is not forbidden to redistribute it. We can keep the image of a sharing center in mind rather than that of a hermetic chest.

More wealth or income generally equates to impacting the lives of more people, which implies a notion of sharing; something which all entrepreneurs know.

A world-renowned actor earns more than a lesser-known actor because of the number of spectators he touches; he makes more people happy. All sales systems are related, in terms of success, to the number of people who benefit from the product being sold.

The multiplication of money for us is relative to the number of lives we improve by adding value to them. It is from there that a financial return can take place. This notion of *mutual benefit* is essential. The purpose of this book is to make massive progress in all areas without harming others.

It is also essential to remember that the level to which we can help others is directly related to our financial means, both on a small and large scale. To bring food to India or Africa, we need planes and abundant means. The more money we have, the more money we can give to those who don't have or help them in different ways.

A wealthy person has a double advantage that can benefit those who are disadvantaged; they have more means to help others, and they demonstrate that it is possible to achieve prosperity. This can be very motivating.

Money is not only a product or a means of exchange, it is also a concrete result and a measure that determines our level of confidence in this area.

All these points can be defined by asking questions like the following:

- When you walk into a store, do you consider purchases according to your desire or your means?
- Do you focus on the product or its price?
- Do you have enough money to do all you want?
- Do you have enough money to help your loved ones and improve their lives?
- Do you have enough money to give to those most in need?
- Do you travel a lot?
- Do you often go to restaurants?
- Do you have enough money to have everything you want?
- Etc.

Improving your confidence is a sure way to improve your finances, and the following story illustrates what a human being can do.

Aristotle Onassis was a young Greek born in 1906 in Smyrna, Turkey, in the comfort of a wealthy family. His father made his fortune in commerce, and young Aristotle grew up in a large house, surrounded by servants.

Used to comfort, he was carefree and relaxed, he spent more time at the pool or tennis court than in the classroom, and he gave more of his attention to his girlfriends than to his homework. He never finished school, much to the chagrin of his father, who never stopped belittling and criticizing him.

At the age of sixteen, young "Ari" seemed well on his way to leading a peaceful and idle life.

Up to this point in the story, nothing seems to illustrate what we have been talking about so far, such as the power of will.

Yet, six months later, his destiny tragically turned hellish. The Turkish army invaded, destroyed and burned his town, then seized his parents' house and took their property. They massacred half of his family before his very eyes, as well as the servants, and he was sent to a prison camp with the few survivors. All that they had left was the clothes on their backs.

It seems difficult to find oneself in a more desperate situation.

Our young friend was born in a well-off environment— he had never made any effort, he did not know the powerful motivating factor of hunger, and he was ultra-traumatized, imprisoned, totally destitute and without any education. Who would bet on his chances in that moment?

For those who do not know the rest, here is a summary. Onassis first manages, thanks to his interpersonal skills, to obtain a pass to leave the prison camp. He comes back a little later and succeeds in finding a new trick to get his father out and evacuate him to Greece by boat.

Then, at the age of seventeen, he left on his own for Argentina without a penny. There, he worked a lot of odd jobs. With his savings, he bought tobacco and sold it at a profit. His business grew rapidly, leading him to earn his first million dollars— the equivalent of 14 million dollars today— by the age of twenty-three.

Two years later, he bought six large freighters on credit and developed a sea freight business. All his life, he, like many Greeks, remained passionate about the sea, and in 1937, at the age of thirty, he had built the largest oil tanker in the world.

At a time when aviation was expanding and everyone was turning away from maritime transport, Ari invested and bought cheap boats which he transformed into supertankers to transport oil. He was the first to understand that the development of the automobile and aeronautics industries would require large quantities of oil. He thus put into action the saying: during a gold rush, sell shovels.

He had quickly become the richest man in the world. When he was not working, he was also very influential and socially successful in orchestrating worldly events. It is he who established the jet-set society as we know it today. He almost became the owner of Monaco, through one of his company, "Les Bains de Mer", and it was at this time that he married off Prince Rainier of Monaco to Grace Kelly. This gives us an idea of his level of influence, which his fortune alone is not enough to explain.

He measured 5 feet 4 inches— very far from the standards of male beauty— but this would not prevent him from being surrounded all his life by the most beautiful women (it should be noted that this was already the case before he made his fortune ...), and in 1968, he married Jacqueline Kennedy; indisputably the most prominent woman of the time.

Once during an interview, when a journalist asked him how he had been so successful with such a physique, Onassis answered with a subtle pirouette: "You're wrong, I'm as handsome as Croesus". This sentiment demonstrates the truth is the fact that everything is "in the head"; it is a question of belief and self-image.

Onassis knew that he could do anything. He had no limits, and that's where his fabulous odyssey was born. But genetically, his constitution was the same as ours.

Key points of the chapter:

- ☑ Our results are the outward expression of our inner image.
- ☑ Our attitude and behaviors are results.
- ☑ Our level of happiness and health are results.
- ☑ The qualities of our family, social and professional relationships are results.
- ☑ The quality of our work or the fact that we don't have one is a result.
- ☑ Our occupations, the way we use our moments of relaxation, are also results.

CHAPTER 5
EVOLUTION

> *"Most people tiptoe through their lives,*
> *without taking any risks, in order to*
> *reach their graves safely"*
>
> Earl Nightingale

If you take a frog and put it in a pan of hot water, it will immediately jump out and escape, but if the same frog is placed in cold water and boiled, it will go numb and stay there until it dies without even trying to escape.

The parallel with our lives is interesting: we sometimes endure small inconveniences on a daily basis so that, when they accumulate, we end up accepting intolerable things. This phenomenon of progressive adaptation illustrates how habits work.

It therefore seems preferable to reflect regularly in order to make the necessary changes, rather than waiting until the tolerance threshold is exceeded, or until rock bottom is reached before going back up.

Habits and comfort zones are intimately linked. They are essential refuge values for the human being who lacks confidence and tries to never leave what is comfortable.

As the writer Jean Dutourd says, "Habit transforms chores into pleasures and pleasures into chores, that is its virtue and vice". This process exists both at the individual level (e.g. in the case of addictions) and collectively, masked under the labels of, "traditions," or "culture," which are nothing more than mass habits.

In the past, women were forbidden from competing in many sports competitions such as the Boston Marathon, for example. This was not to the liking of Kathrine Switzer, who registered for the marathon in 1967 and simply gave her initials in order to obtain the right to participate. Her act of will and her physical capacities— for which many men would envy her— allowed many sporting traditions to evolve. By typing her name into an internet search engine, you will find pictures of her during the race, and of the organizer acting like a fool as he runs behind her to try to snatch her bib.

The submission of man to his habits is a curse. It has its origins in the unconscious fear of losing what one already possesses, and in the fear of the unknown.

Habits often set in without our realizing it, in a very insidious way, and much like the heat in the frog's pan.

Doing something we know how to do because we have already done it makes us feel safe and comfortable.

This is the great challenge in coaching: no progress can be made for those who are not aware of this and refuse to face the feeling of discomfort that comes with new behavior.

For this reason, we must set goals for ourselves that seem out of reach in order to force us to get out of our tranquility and do uncomfortable things. It is not possible to evolve and obtain better results by playing it safe.

We must plan our path and then jump into the unknown if we want to evolve. Progress can only come as a result of that jump. Comfort will return when this new behavior becomes a habit and it will signal us to move forward again.

One of the laws of nature is permanent evolution and change. This is the law of growth, and forward motion is our essence.

It starts from the moment of our birth. We are already in a constant state of evolution and for this reason we sleep and feed ourselves permanently. From the very first days, everything is based on progression with the goal of succeeding in doing new things.

When we learn to speak, we try again and again, doing a little better each time until we succeed. Then we keep trying, and eventually speaking becomes automatic. We no longer need to think about it and mastery has been accomplished.

When learning to walk, we fall and bump hundreds of times, but it would not occur to us for a second to give up.

With walking barely mastered, we want to run, then we want to run faster.

Each step builds on the previous one. We climb and want to climb higher. Then we travel further and further.

The watchwords are *development* and *constant progression*.

Throughout our existence, we always reach for *more*, and that's very healthy. Phrases such as, "You should be satisfied with what you have," "Stop dreaming," should be banished forever. Yet this is the kind of nonsense that is heard from generation to generation, without the people who repeat it ever having really thought about what it means; recommending deprivation to one's neighbor.

We must never accept incentives to renunciation, even if they come (often) from well-meaning people, who are mistaken more by ignorance than by malice.

Our goal is simply to *improve*. "The ideal of life is not the hope of becoming perfect, it is the will to be better and better," Emerson said.

As such, the examples of Helen Keller and Laura Bridgman are extraordinary.

Helen and Laura were born fifty years apart in the United States and their fates were similar; they both fell ill in their very first years of life and became blind, deaf, and mute.

At first, they had the same reaction in isolation from the outside world, with both becoming out of control. It was impossible for their parents to communicate with them. Often, they would spit out the food they were offered, throw terrible tantrums, hit people who approached them, and throw objects in all directions.

Laura was placed in an adapted institute, and a specialist came to take care of Helen at home. The beginnings were long and difficult as the girls did not want to abide by any rules and responded systematically with anger and violence. The forms of learning they received, however, gradually helped them to improve their terrible condition and even to experience joy.

In both cases, they learned in the same way. The instructors began by placing objects in the girls' hands, after which they would tap the corresponding letters of the alphabet into the girls' palms to name the objects. One thing led to another and they began to learn the alphabet this way. Many years later, Laura and Helen graduated and gave speeches and lectures to give hope to those around them and explain how they did it.

As soon as the phase of progression stops or the activity ceases, quite naturally, a phase of regression occurs. There is no intermediate phase. To be convinced of this, all you must do is take an object and throw it in the air. When it stops rising, it begins to fall back down.

The phenomenon is the same for humans, animals, plants and minerals: at the end of the growth phase, regression or even decomposition occurs.

Let's take the example of a bodybuilder: if he stops training, he will immediately observe muscular regression.

For this to not happen, he will have to continue practicing his sessions without respite. Intellectually, the same thing happens. A chess player, a mathematician, or a scientist cannot give up their practice while remaining at the same level. Like a snowman that you must build by constantly adding snow, because the moment you stop, it starts to melt.

This is why retirement can be destructive for those who do not substitute their work with other activities. Without activity, we get bored and quickly become dull. Becoming satisfied with inactivity once we are rested is a very bad idea. Wanting to stay at level without practice or moving forward is impossible, for the simple reason that inertia does not exist in nature as we now know. It is impossible to freeze anything; *evolution* and *protection* are opposite.

Our capacity for action lies in the choice of direction, because, when looking for neutral, we always find reverse.

Even a body in a coffin is in motion: not inert but decomposing. When this phase is completed, the dust will continue its transformation.

As the chemist Antoine Lavoisier taught us, "Nothing is lost, nothing is created, everything is transformed". If we take a block of granite and observe it under a microscope, we will see that it is not inert; everything is in motion. Matter is energy and it is in permanent vibration. From the smallest atom to the largest planet, nothing rests. Everything in the universe moves.

Key points of the chapter:

- ☑ Our habits slowly and surely invade and numb us.

- ☑ They take control of our lives and become unconscious.

- ☑ To gain awareness, we must have the courage to jump into the unknown.

- ☑ Comfort and evolution don't mix.

- ☑ After the progression comes the regression.

- ☑ Man is made to evolve.

CHAPTER 6
OUR THOUGHTS

> *'Reign over your mind or it will control you"*
>
> Horace (10 B.C.)

The thoughts that occupy our mind are like seeds we plant in the fertile soil that is our unconscious.

We are free to choose our thoughts, just as we would be free to choose the seeds we decide to sow. If we plant flower seeds, we will get flowers. If we plant nothing, or if we plant weeds, weeds will grow.

We freely choose our thoughts and maintain them in full consciousness. No one person or external element can influence our thoughts without our consent.

We need to take as much care in filtering what we let into our brains as we do in filtering what we let into our bodies during our meals. We know the consequences of ingesting toxic or harmful products. Concerning thoughts, the process is the same; they take control of our unconscious mind, and that's why we must use our brain as a filter.

For Marcus Aurelius "a man's life is based on his thoughts."

Our thoughts condition our attitude and behavior and our actions are the direct result. They can make our life a dream or a nightmare. Our outside world is only a reflection of what is going on in our mind.

We are in control of the situation. We are the ones who are in charge, and it is in our interest to make a rigorous selection, because the quality of our life depends on the choice we make of our thoughts.

The laws of nature are extremely precise, as we have seen; when something happens, there is always a reason for it, whether we know it or not. Luck and chance do not exist. These are two words that man has invented to give a justification for what he cannot explain. They are comfortable illusions that serve as excuses. Unfortunately, these excuses absolve us of all responsibility and infantilize us.

Understanding that the spirit precedes matter and that the quality of our thoughts creates the quality of our life is not mysticism— quite the contrary. Mysticism would be to believe that elements of our life are accidentally created by some external power.

As Shakespeare said, "The fault, my dear Brutus, is within us, it does not come from the stars".

We must choose and maintain positive and motivating thoughts to improve our lives. This principle is very simple, but not easy to apply; it is a habit to acquire. Be assured that this acquisition is possible; it is a matter of training and many people succeed in it. It is the quality of their results that makes them recognizable.

It is not, of course, a question of thinking in terms of fighting our impulses, nor of repressing our instincts which would cause tension and prove to be very limiting. Rather, it is about cultivating our optimism by becoming more aware of our power.

This is perfectly illustrated in the following anecdote: a very important and influential man enters a restaurant with his son and says to him: "you see my son; you must have the attitude of the person who owns this restaurant". The son, not very convinced, replies that this is not easy to do and that if he had his father's power the task would be much easier. His father, at this point, taught him a lesson he would never forget by explaining that it is the way of thinking that leads to success and that it is not success that leads to the way of thinking.

This is so misunderstood and important that I will repeat it again: We create our universe by our thoughts, not by our actions. It is not our actions that create our universe, it is our thoughts that create our universe.

If we focus our thoughts on doubt we will fail, if we focus our thoughts on success we will succeed. This is the recipe for success summed up in a short sentence, simple as that, but not so easy to do...

The quality of our thoughts leads us to a higher universe and the technique used is only a detail.

Thoughts crystallize and then solidify into their tangible equivalent. A positive person who sees good everywhere can be assured that he or she is creating a positive world.

Thoughts can be constructive and increase our confidence and awareness, or they can be destructive and decrease them.

It is obvious that all the thoughts that keep us away from others and which are the source of resentment— anger, rivalry, jealousy, etc.— will paralyze us if we accept them. The good news is that by improving our confidence, we quickly become free of these types of feelings.

Metaphysics teaches us that we are all one unique consciousness, and that all forms of separation go against our purpose.

Psychoanalysis, for its part, teaches us that all the judgments we make about others are as illusory as those we make about ourselves (as we saw in the first two chapters).

These judgments we make about others are called *projections*. For Freud, they are "defense mechanisms in the form of transporting outward from one's own psychic space". Shakespeare had already declared, more soberly, four hundred years earlier, "To judge others is to judge oneself".

These mental behaviors are unconscious, of course. The subject expels by pointing out in others, the qualities, defects, or feelings that he refuses to perceive in himself.

Any judgment of others would be a projection.

It goes like this: if Paul says when talking to Peter, "You're stupid, you're just a jerk," it reveals that Paul is insecure about his own intelligence, and subconsciously uses Peter as a subject to allow his own complex to surface.

It is sometimes more comfortable for us to criticize others than to open our eyes, but this attitude solves nothing and is double-edged because it does not deceive the initiated.

The emotion attached to a projection is all the stronger for the victim the more he or she feels concerned. If one is called a microbe, for example, we can assume that tall people will be the least affected... When strong emotions, such as anger or fury get involved, the judgment becomes very suspicious.

Also, judgments, or even insults, must be seen for what they are; confessions of weakness on the part of those who make them, and therefore, an indication of suffering. Socrates said, "It is better to suffer the insult than to commit it".

The lesson to be learned when we are "victims" of a projection (i.e. when we "detect" a defect in someone else), is to consider this feeling to be an alarm inviting us to work on the corresponding trait within ourselves.

A psychologist friend of mine explained to me the following exercise that he makes his new patients do. He asks them to take a sheet of paper and divide it in half by drawing a vertical line. He then makes them write the first five qualities that come to mind in the right-hand column, and five defects in the left-hand column. He then tells them to hold the sheet of paper at arm's length and consider it a mirror. He finds in it a good basis to start working.

Of course, projections can also be positive. Lovers see many positive qualities in their loved one— we always find a lot of them in people we like and that's fine.

Contrary to projections revealing negative values, those based on noble feelings benefit everyone.

When we welcome a limiting thought, a subtle mechanism is often put in place to direct our actions in the direction necessary to justify and rationalize it for our ego.

If we think that the world and the people in it are malicious, we will subconsciously rearrange to surround ourselves with malicious people and actions to confirm our beliefs. We will not notice the many acts of kindness that occur right under our noses.

The more emotionally-charged our thoughts are, the greater their impact will be, as we saw in the previous section on the unconscious.

We can't stop these thoughts from invading our brains all the time. A kind of permanent monologue is going on inside us. This mental conversation that we are constantly having is as much a human constant as the need for oxygen, food, or water. Unless in altered states like meditation, we can't stop it, but we can direct it in a positive way, and in this way, we can maintain a state of mental harmony.

Are we thinking about our future or are we thinking about our past? In other words, are we thinking about what we can change or are we thinking about what we cannot change?

It is smart to think in positive terms and not to focus too much on events for which we do not have the capacity to intervene or influence. Lamenting the harm done by an economic crisis or an earthquake is understandable, but useless not to say harmful.

On the other hand, thinking about our dispute with our cousin is not the same thing, in as much as we can act to resolve the conflict. Our thinking, of course, must be constructive and lead us to act.

An experiment was conducted with young, skilled chess players. Two groups of players of equivalent level were asked to watch documentaries with very heavy subjects (wars, disasters etc.). No instructions were given to the first group, whereas the participants in the second group were warned that they would be shown difficult images and should therefore struggle to repress the feelings derived from them. These players were then brought together and given difficult and complex problems to solve.

The researchers found that the second group which had spent energy trying to suppress their emotions were much less successful than the first group.

Some lessons can be learned from this. Repressing negative thoughts make us weaker. Our reserves of energy are not inexhaustible, after all.

The thoughts we must also get rid of at all costs are the very harmful thoughts of fear and worry. They too destroy self-image and are the source of many disappointments.

We must ask ourselves whether we spend our time thinking about what we want— imagining the successful realization of our projects— or if we spend our time thinking about what we don't want— worrying that our projects won't come true. In the latter case, activates without any doubts an unconscious dynamic of failure.

Bad thoughts are the equivalent to harboring an unwanted guest, giving it energy, and cultivating a state of stress. This situation of fragility can have many consequences, both psychological and physical.

It is not possible to accept, or nurture limiting thoughts or emotions and expect good results.

The information that comes to us every day from different sources also gives rise to thoughts. Whether it comes from our relationships or from the media, it is essential to be able to manage it in such a way that it does not have a negative impact on us.

This does not mean living in denial, or becoming insensitive, but it does not make sense to maintain a negative feeling more than is necessary. This is even more important since the unconscious does not have the capacity to reject what it feels, as we have already seen. It accepts without distinction, all our emotions, before externalizing them in one way or another.

A few years ago, something very interesting happened in Texas. One of the roads between Dallas and Houston— lined with telegraph poles every one hundred and fifty feet— became particularly slippery in rainy weather.

Authorities noted that a significant percentage of accidents involved vehicles colliding with poles, despite the low probability of such an accident due to the size of the gaps between the poles. They concluded that this was due to the poor placement of the poles and they shifted all of them.

However, subsequent accidents produced the same results with most cars, once again, crashing into the poles.

We have seen that the subconscious does not know negative formulas such as "avoid" (remember the green hippopotamus). Also, it is obvious that motorists who were run off the road and tried to *avoid* the poles ended up running into them since they had these "poles" in mind!

We bring into our lives what we have in mind; This is the great secret.

I know a lot of people around me who want to quit smoking, for example. Keeping in mind the idea of suppressing tobacco sustains the desire to smoke.

A better approach would be to imagine living fully.

To avoid something, it is better to fill our mind with its opposite

On a more amusing note, if we think that wearing black pants is bad luck, we're more likely to slip on a banana peel the day we wear them.

The human being prefers to receive a few blows rather than admit that he is wrong. Pride and reflection often go hand in hand rather poorly.

In this last example, it is easy to avoid buying black pants, but if we believe that we always catch a cold when we are in a room with an open window, it is better to get rid of this belief. In this case, we may catch a cold quite often.

Key points of the chapter:

- ☑ We are what we think about.

- ☑ Our thoughts condition our attitude.

- ☑ The quality of our thoughts determines the quality of our life.

- ☑ Thinking about success is the first step.

- ☑ Any judgment we make about others would reveal what we unconsciously think about ourselves.

- ☑ Any concern is limiting.

- ☑ Any thought against others, whether conscious or subconscious, is both a cause and a source of suffering.

CHAPTER 7
THE NOTIONS OF INTERIOR AND EXTERIOR

"If your five senses tell you that you're not going to succeed in life, imagine a sixth"

Mahamat Haroun

We perceive the world mainly with five of our senses (sight, vision, smell, taste, and touch) beginning at birth. As soon as we are old enough to understand what we are told, those around us reinforce our tendency to pay attention to our five senses with phrases such as, "Look at what you are doing," "Listen to what I am telling you," "Stop touching that," and many other similar suggestions.

This leads us "naturally" to consider everything around us as a prerequisite for our actions, and to adapt our thinking to it. We thus become dependent on external circumstances, we build our personality from this state of allegiance, and we end up reacting rather than acting.

The man or woman of action is replaced by the man or woman of *reaction*.

The natural order is reversed; we are subjugated, we kneel before the external events that dictate our lives, and it is from this position that we make our decisions.

Another misdeed of this dependence on circumstances—whatever the content— is that when what surrounds us does not correspond to our expectations, it creates doubt in our minds.

Difficulties do not arise from obstacles, but from the mental barriers they create. An obstacle can always be crossed or bypassed.

Once we become aware of this process, it becomes possible to change this. We begin by asking ourselves if we want to control our lives or not. We will never be able to do anything worthwhile or interesting if we pay attention to the things around us. This is obvious if we think about it and if we want to move forward.

Attention can either be drawn from the outside or directed from the inside. It is directed from within when we deliberately choose our goals based on our tastes and desires.

Thinking about one's real desires and acting accordingly is, despite appearances, difficult, but it is the price of success and many people succeed every day. The stronger our desire is, the easier it is for this form of thinking to maintain itself, which is why adopting other people's thoughts is never a good motivator.

By first defining our intentions, we will avoid being influenced externally. Then, and only then, will we be able to evaluate external elements to establish our path. We will not adapt our objectives to the circumstances. What we will adapt is the way to achieve them.

Anyone who wants to open a school for example, without knowing how to go about it is not going to stop there. He will find out more information, fill in his gaps, surround himself with teachers and move towards his goal.

Anyone who cannot afford a car today will not stop at this obstacle. He will think about finding financing, and then he will act to achieve this result.

Our five senses are there to inform us, but above all we have six superior faculties that we must rely on if we want to see our desires and goals realized.

These faculties function like muscles; the more we use them, the more they will develop. They are the will, the intuition, the reason, the memory, the perception, and the imagination. These faculties are specific to man, contrary to the five senses, which all animals possess.

We must use and abuse these six superior faculties if we want to improve our existence and mark our difference from the animal kingdom; more so since in certain sectors we are forced to bow respectfully before the animal's superiority.

Have you ever witnessed the birth of a horse or another animal? Have you seen how quickly it gets up, leaps, and starts living its life? Let's compare it to a human baby: how many months do we lie in total dependency? How many years do we have to be fed and assisted?

The reason for this is that humans have these faculties which allow them to create their own environment; they are not designed to adapt.

Let us now address one after the other these six faculties through which we can act from the inside out (and not from the outside in). I repeat: these six faculties are like muscles. By making them work, we make them more efficient.

Intuition

Intuition is a precious inner guide that can help us and often prevent us from making mistakes. It will guide us without having to reason or use logic.

It allows us to decode the energy emitted by those around us behind appearances. When someone is not sincere, their body and their thoughts are not in agreement— they are not in harmony. There is a rupture that impacts the "vibrations" felt by the intuitive and makes this person uncomfortable.

Sometimes it is a good idea to clear our mind and discern what signals our body is sending us when faced with an event, a person, or a decision.

The worst enemy of intuition is the mind, and its best ally is calmness. It is in this state that we learn to develop intuition, because it needs this kind of space to be able to surface.

Memory

Memory will allow us to cross-reference and select information from our "database" in order to replicate the actions that work for us and avoid those that do not serve us.

Memorization also requires calmness, and a minimal healthy lifestyle necessary for it to work; training the brain and exercises are vital to cultivate and develop good memorization. There are many books and methods based on mental combinations and associations of ideas which are very effective. I have personally seen people perform "miracles" during seminars; reciting passages that other participants themselves chose out from hundreds of pages.

Reason

The word "reason" comes etymologically from the word *ratio*, which means, "measurement," or, "calculation". It is reason that allows us to make our choices.

We can reason away from prejudices, impulses, and emotions. Here again, training is essential; we return to the importance of the acquired versus the innate.

Let's take two identical people and raise one of them in front of reality TV programs and video games while the other one grows up reading great authors and we'll see the difference in the quality of their reasoning.

Will

Will alone could be the subject of an entire book. It is related to perseverance, and often marks the difference between success and failure. Thomas Edison and his engineers, who developed the light bulb, failed thousands of times over the years, but they were never discouraged because they saw their failures as calls to double their efforts. Eventually they succeeded and changed the world.

Let us note in passing that they, "started from the inside," from a seemingly delusional idea, without concern for external circumstances. They started again after each unsuccessful attempt, remaining concentrated and convinced that the real failure would be to give up.

Willpower is linked to the ability to concentrate and is reinforced from success to success. It is like a magnifying glass that unifies the sun's rays and concentrates them into a single point.

Will allows one to resist the call of immediate pleasure, which is often counterproductive.

It can be illustrated, here again, by the example of food: have you noticed how the tastiest things are almost always the unhealthiest? Without willpower, we would be in worse shape.

A very interesting experiment was conducted in an American university in the 1960s. Experimenters placed a candy in front of each student in a small class and told them that if they waited an hour before eating it, the teacher would come back and give them a second one. Then they left the students alone and filmed them. Some resisted, others did not.

Researchers revisited these same students a few years later and found that those who had resisted the temptation were doing much better in life in general than the others.

It is beneficial for us to get used to making our decisions upstream, reasoning once and for all, and leaving no room for doubt. Like when we follow a diet let's decide once and for all to do it. This way we will no longer think before each dish to decide whether we should eat it or not. The question will have been decided in advance.

Perception

Perception is an individual faculty with a highly variable geometry. As with thoughts, our perception depends on us. It is each of us who chooses our reactions to events.

Let's take a few examples:

A hunter and his young daughter are walking in a forest and come across a rabbit. The little girl wants to take it in her arms, hug it, and bring it home to cherish it, while the hunter wants to kill it to eat it.

An old farmer lives with his two sons who help him cultivate his land. One day, one of the sons breaks his leg, and this event is immediately perceived as a great misfortune. These people are not rich; they must work all day and this son will not be able to help his father and brother for a while. The next day, the farmer sees soldiers disembark with the aim of enlisting all able-bodied men to go to war. The wounded son is obviously exempted. The misfortune of the day before turned out to have a positive consequence.

Let's take the example at the end of the first chapter: someone on the street smiles at a stranger of the opposite sex who looks away and does not smile back. This person may think that the stranger looked away out of disdain or worse, because he or she found them ugly. They may also think, on the contrary, that the stranger is very interested in them, but that he or she did not dare to smile back out of shyness.

There is no truth. Everyone has their own, and there are as many truths as there are individuals. "Everyone is right from his or her own point of view, but it is not impossible that everyone is wrong," said Gandhi, yet without a smile.

What is important to understand is the impact from either a positive or a negative perspective. One is stimulating, the other is demotivating.

Imagination

To end on a high note, let's look at our sixth faculty: imagination.

Napoleon said of imagination that it rules the world and that nothing great can be done without it. Einstein said that imagination was more important than knowledge and intelligence, and that if logic could take us from point A to point B, imagination could take us everywhere.

No progress or scientific breakthrough could have taken place without it, and we would still be eating with our hands, and without plates or chairs to sit on.

There is no man-made object on this planet, from the smallest utensil to the Seven Wonders of the World, that has not first been a product of the imagination, in the form of a thought.

As already mentioned, the distressing expression uttered by so many people that "We shouldn't take our dreams for reality" is immeasurably stupid. The mistake is not dreaming, but rather, not acting in order to make our dreams come true.

Sometimes we do even worse, often using our imagination in an unfavorable way as we have seen in evoking unpleasant thoughts, or worrying, for example. Worrying is using our imagination to create negative events. How absurd!

Imagining positive events requires no more energy than imagining negative ones.

We must use our imagination to know what we want, and to stay focused on it. This too has already been written, but in order to potentiate our *self-image*, repetition is mandatory; our brain must be bombarded a thousand times with the same truths so that it is permanently altered.

Key points of the chapter:

☑ We define our goals by looking at our desires, not our circumstances.

☑ Any obstacle can be managed in one way or another if doubt is removed.

☑ Let us learn to cultivate our superior faculties: intuition, memory, reason, will, perception, imagination.

☑ These six faculties have brought about all human achievements.

☑ Our perception is our choice which defines our universe.

☑ Our imagination allows us to define our objectives.

CHAPTER 8
GRATITUDE

"It is not happiness that fills us with gratitude, it is gratitude that fills us with happiness"

David Steindl-Rast

Gratitude and *recognition* are ideal attitudes that we should strive for. It is interesting to note how close these two words, "gratitude," and "attitude," are. In this case, gratitude is a superior attitude.

Gratitude is a powerful, transformative, and necessary feeling that is sure to lead to success. The more we can feel grateful in all circumstances, the more we will rise, and the more we will elevate our self-image at the same time.

We must strive to feel gratitude in all circumstances, both good and bad.

This feeling puts us in the right frame of mind to reap many benefits. Good things come from the quality of our attitude and actions.

If someone offers us something and we don't show our gratitude, we might not receive anything more from that person.

The laws of nature are the same as those that govern relations between individuals; there is nothing magical. For life to have beautiful surprises in store for us, we must also feel gratitude towards it. To do the opposite would be like closing a window at the back of a house, preventing the flow of air from flowing freely.

This feeling is equivalent to being on a good frequency. By feeling recognition, we focus on the best aspects of things, which is the necessary condition for positivity to gradually become the content of our world.

In addition to putting us on a good wavelength, gratitude is a strong disposition.

Many years ago, during a war, my father was driving around in his car and stopped to pick up a young hitchhiker who was walking along the road, obviously in a state of total destitution. The unlucky sixteen-year-old, whose name was Jacques, was going to the front to help his comrades. My father took him in and gave him some comfort and human compassion that day.

Jacques never forgot. They continued to see each other for more than fifty years and all his life, Jacques felt an unfailing gratitude to my father.

They haven't been with us for a long time, but I can still testify to the power of this feeling.

Conversely, when we feel dissatisfied, we focus on the wrong side of things and we lose altitude. Our world and the quality of what we harvest decline in turn.

This attitude is valid for events as well as for people. When we are angry at someone, we hurt ourselves. Bad thoughts penalize those who give them, not those who receive them. Resentment or bitterness are self-inflicted poisons. In fact, it is like throwing dust on a fan that is in front of us.

Let's try to get used to seeing only the good side of people, and they will repay us well. We are *part* of nature, and therefore, must have faith in the principle of reciprocity *between* ourselves and nature.

For my part, when I find myself in a static situation— traffic or waiting for an appointment— I try to think about positive things. It's a mental tool and an interesting exercise. It is good to take everything in this matter; a smile I receive, a material object I like, a past or future event, it doesn't matter. The objective is to find oneself in a certain mental state.

I also remember, in the same vein, a friend of mine named Gene. He once told me that when he talked about people, he always tried to say only good things about them. His wife and children knew the rule. At the dinner table, during meals, they always spoke highly of people, emphasizing their qualities— it was a family rule.

He told me that it had changed their lives. His acquaintances were much more positive towards him even though they didn't know how he valued them.

There are many things that our rationality cannot yet explain.

A study was conducted in the United States in the 80s to investigate whether there was a link between experiencing gratitude and longevity of life; not an easy thing to do! It was necessary to find people who were quite similar and who lived the same way— breathing the same air, with the same jobs, etc.— and to be able to rely on statistics kept over time.

Eventually, researchers found a convent in which archives had been kept for generations. The young women who arrived at the convent at the age of twenty had to write a letter introducing themselves and their lives. They did the same thing every ten years for the rest of their lives. One hundred and fifty years of autobiographical letters and medical records were kept in the convent.

Scientists studied all these documents, considering the content of the vocabulary and quantifying the nature of the words used to express wonder, optimism, or gratitude. They then correlated the "density of gratitude" in these women with their health status and life span. They found that the more words they used to express gratitude from the age of twenty, the longer the women had lived. They even managed to quantify this "longer life," estimating that the women expressing more gratitude had gained, on average, seven years of life expectancy over their sisters.

This research has obviously been reproduced in more common contexts and, in all environments has arrived ate same result.

Being able to add a few years to one's life seems like a good thing, especially since in this case we are talking about years of happiness!

Sandy Gallagher has invented the word, "gratituding," and she has an excellent trick to use it: she instructs people to mentally select people who bother them— famous or from their personal circle— and imagine sending love to them. She tells them to imagine themselves hugging them, congratulating them, and laughing with them. Try to do the same: think of people that might worry you, and imagine yourself laughing with them, and visualize mutual congratulations. This can be an effective trick to instantly change your frequency.

These little mental tricks, sometimes quite useful, are called "rituals" when they are performed on a regular basis. This is the word coaches use. Generally, when they are psychological, they are preferably practiced in the morning when waking up, or when falling asleep in the evening, because the mind is calmer and more receptive at these times than during the day.

There are as many possibilities as there are people, and everyone repeats "rituals": brushing your teeth, for example, is one of them. Others eat a kiwi, practice meditation, or take a piece of paper and write down ten reasons for being grateful.

These rituals are variable, but while researching the subject, I was very surprised at the number of famous people having different rituals daily in order to be more effective. Here are a few names to convince you of this, among hundreds of a very heterogeneous list: Joan of Arc, Ludwig von Beethoven, Mahatma Gandhi, Leonardo da Vinci, Victor Hugo, Honoré de Balzac, Oscar Wilde, Charles Dickens, Stephen King, Pablo Picasso, René Magritte, Steve Jobs, Richard Branson, and Elon Musk all have, or had, small daily habits.

A popular ritual nowadays in the United States and practiced by many people worldwide is to write one or two sentences with the non-dominant hand. Not as silly as it sounds, since this gesture helps develop new neurons.

Gratitude must also apply in bad times. It's not as easy, but it's more powerful. Compare this to joy, for example: would we say of someone that he is a joyful being if he is not joyful in all circumstances?

We are who we are today because of the events we have experienced so far, both good and bad. Beginning to regret the painful moments amounts to a kind of self-denial, and this has a negative impact on our self-image. It is not possible to truly love yourself while rejecting the experiences that have shaped you. The past is over and cannot be changed. We must accept everything with gratitude to not indirectly diminish ourselves.

We are familiar with the two common sense proverbs: "To something bad is good," and, "Misfortune is a source of experience". Many thinkers teach us that if we are confronted with misfortunes in our lives, it is not by hazard, but for the sole purpose of learning how to deal with them with greatness in order to evolve. Turning failure into teaching is one way to eliminate it.

No matter which area affects us, these trials will be repeated in the same area until we learn to respond favorably and take advantage of the lessons learned.

This helps us to understand how some people face similar problems day after day, without being able to overcome them. Being aware of this and focusing on the right aspect of events is the remedy. This brings us back to our precious faculty of perception.

Key points of the chapter:

- ☑ Gratitude is a higher frequency.
- ☑ It is a powerful force of attraction.
- ☑ This state is valid for good things as well as bad things.
- ☑ Let's integrate it with other little tricks that make us more efficient.
- ☑ Tests are lessons, not obstacles.

CHAPTER 9
RESPONSIBLE OR A VICTIM

"A sense of responsibility is the price of greatness"

Winston Churchill

Along with the feeling of gratitude, there is a second behavior that allows us to considerably improve our self-image, increase our self-confidence, and achieve a high degree of freedom.

It's about a *sense of responsibility* and an absolute refusal to make excuses.

When we endorse this feeling 100%, in all circumstances, and regardless of external elements or the actions of others, our life is transformed. When we are completely free from seeking approval from others, we feel the breath of liberty. We become autonomous and focus our attention on our own judgment and actions rather than those of others.

The first area in which we are responsible is that of our attitude and reactions to events. We have the option to act, or to suffer by positioning ourselves as victims.

Unfortunately, we have not been conditioned to take responsibility for events, as we have all been looking for excuses since our early childhood. This is normal and in no way condemnable until we reach a certain age. It is precisely the characteristic of childhood to not take responsibility; that is what adults are there for.

Where this attitude is problematic is when it eventually becomes a habit. Many adults can't get rid of it and get stuck at this childhood stage.

Another fascinating human phenomenon is hidden under the term "confabulation," which consists of inventing story posteriori to justify an act. The objective being, of course, to reject responsibility and blame others or circumstances.

For example, a person stumbles in the street. she will explain to those around her, even though she was the only one to fall there, that the ground was slippery.

Another example is when a person is caught digging through documents that do not belong to them. When they are caught, they will claim that they were doing a favor by putting the documents in order. They may even take advantage of the situation and blame the person for their lack of organization! These dishonest games we play to justify our actions, when we are supposed to be adults, seem fascinating to me.

I know someone who borrowed an important sum of money from someone else and never paid it back. The subject came up much later, and she justified herself by explaining that she had borrowed the money in order to reduce the lender's wealth and lower her taxes! I am not making up this pathological story, I promise you that it is, unfortunately, true.

Confabulation is often unconscious; We must be very vigilant. Many people play these kinds of games to convince themselves of something as well. When a person speaks harshly to another because they are in a bad mood, the first person will say that they are right because the second person needed to be shaken. In fact, they will have spoken aggressively to do the person a favor.

Very funny! But burying one's head in the sand and telling stories is not a recommended way to gain respect or develop a strong self-image...

The other similar phenomenon that is often grafted onto the absence of responsibility is the need for instant gratification. An equally immature behavior is privileging an immediate fleeting pleasure to the detriment of a real and lasting benefit. This behavior is the twin brother of positioning oneself as a victim. We find, here again, excellent examples in the relationship to food to help us understand this principle.

Let's have a sweet treat— a Mars bar, perhaps— and a plate of green beans.

A Mars bar is delicious, and the pleasure is immediate (let us salute in passing the talent of these wonderful chemists who work in these multinational corporations to bring us so many sweet flavors). In the short term, our insulin levels are on a roller coaster ride, and in the long term, if we are a frequent consumer, we are simply threatening our health as well as our physical appearance.

Concerning green beans, it is easy to admit that the pleasure is not the same, but the medium, and long-term effects have no negative consequences. These foods will make us high-performing and fit people.

We can also transpose these examples to many fields other than food. So many temptations present themselves to us in life; temptations of immediate, short-term pleasure, and long-term harm. It is a choice we must make; we are free and responsible for our destiny. In fact, life becomes easy if we take the difficult path, and it is difficult if we take the easy path.

Abstinence is difficult, even if it is a source of future positive outcomes. That is why so many of us give in to the easy and immediate pleasures, despite the consequences. This choice has been anchored in our collective memory for millions of years. Indeed, there was a very distant time when, if ever we had food, we were obliged to consume it without delay. Not because we didn't have a refrigerator, but because we risked having our meal snatched away by other members of our tribe or by some animal, and we were happy not to be part of the meal.

Life at that time was so dangerous that we had to immediately take advantage of what we had. We could not protect ourselves as we do today. There were no houses with locks, nor laws to guarantee us a minimum of security. We lived in this way for 99.99% of our human existence. Even two hundred and fifty years ago, life expectancy was not even thirty years; this does not encourage restraint or long-term forecasting!

However, this atavism should not serve as an excuse for not trying. On the contrary, let's try to take advantage of our privileged situation and the advantages it offers us.

We become adults the day we understand that *we* are the cause of our results. Our words and actions must also be congruent.

Without making jokes, the fact that many people make real efforts of imagination to perpetually abdicate their responsibilities is no excuse for doing so.

Some even go so far as to think of themselves as victims of their own beliefs, which is quite a feat.

Responsibility is a choice, and that choice is a key to freedom. Taking responsibility for ourselves and others and seeing ourselves as responsible for our entire existence as well as our results gives us control.

Making this decision is a no-brainer if you think about it a little bit.

When we look for excuses and try to justify our results by blaming events, circumstances, or others, we instantly become a victim. This victimization syndrome is a way of life for some of us.

We devalue ourselves by presenting as a person who depends on the generosity of circumstances or others. We demonstrate that we lack resources. We lose our power by attributing it to some hypothetical external forces.

Our ego, which is hidden behind all this and whose logic is sometimes mysterious, is in fact diminished so as not to appear diminished ...

By playing the victim and blaming those around us, we tyrannize them. We isolate ourselves and suppress any possibility of fulfillment. Imagine the impact on our self-confidence and self-esteem when we resign in this way.

We all have infinitely more respect for a person who systematically takes responsibility for events than for those who spend their time justifying themselves and blaming circumstances.

Collectively, it is the same and that explains the large amount of laws for the society we live in. With greater collective responsibility, we would be less infantilized by all these prohibitions.

The other day, I was washing my hands in the bathroom of a restaurant. There was a sign on the wall explaining how to wash my hands in eight successive points along with explanatory drawings.

We are responsible for many more things than we often think, since we are responsible for our health, our relationships, our job, our occupations, and our lives.

Although it is impossible to control everything, always taking responsibility is the key to liberty. By doing so, we don't waste time justifying, complaining, or accusing, we keep a constructive spirit and remain fully focused on our progress.

The person who gets caught in the rain has the leisure to get angry and to blame the weather and bad luck. In doing so, however, they get into the habit of positioning themselves as victims and are assured that this kind of small inconvenience will happen to them again. Taking responsibility for events puts us in a position to anticipate and manage.

If our apartment is burglarized while we are away on vacation, we can tell ourselves that we were unlucky or dream of mild punishments based on boiling pots and various sharpened cooking utensils, assuming we get our hands on the burglars. But in doing so, we leave the door open—as I might say in this circumstance— to a subsequent burglary. If, on the contrary, we assume our responsibility, we will act so that it doesn't happen again.

A victim cannot create.

One example among a hundred: two friends have lunch together. One complains to the other about catching a cold because the window of the restaurant where he had lunched the day before was open. Why didn't he ask if it was possible for the window to be closed? If it was not possible, why didn't he ask for a different table? It's so simple. Will he do the same thing next time?

Since I started writing this book, I have interviewed a lot of people in many situations, whenever I had the opportunity to do so. I often do this especially with those who inform others of their obligations. Everywhere, there are rules to ensure harmony in society. People follow them, and some pass them on. It can be a policeman, but also a salesperson in a business, a waitress in a restaurant, an organizer at a party, an instructor at a summer camp, and many other cases.

When they give an instruction, I question them on the primary reason for this instruction, taking care not to offend them and making it clear that it is not a question of me judging, but of a desire to understand.

Many tell me that they don't know, or that their boss has asked them to do so. Their number is edifying more than 80%. For a given salary, they execute orders and have them subsequently executed by others without knowing why, and they don't mind. It's terrible! Here again, we must go back to childhood and to the conditioning carried out by their parents, who answered with phrases like, "Because that's how it is".

Another classic, alas, particularly destructive for a child, is emotional blackmail. A little one does something stupid and the father intervenes to tell him, "Don't do this, you'll hurt your mother's feelings". The father doesn't take responsibility for reprimanding the child, and instead, shifts his responsibility to his wife. Additionally, he asks the child, on top of everything else, to behave like an adult... It would be fun if this didn't happen so often. Making a child feel guilty by making him believe that he is a source of suffering for his parents is an unstoppable way to create a burden that he will have a hard time getting rid of.

Here's another story that a doctor friend of mine once told me: it was about two sisters whose mother had ruined their lives due to very severe alcoholism. Their youth was dramatic, and one of them became an alcoholic as well. Followed by a specialist because she was eager to overcome this addiction and to have a normal life, she was unemployed and lived alone. Her other sister was married, had children, had become a lawyer, led a balanced life, and took great care of her sister during difficult times. When the doctor questioned the patient who was drinking, she invariably told him that *following* her mother's example had unfortunately led her to *become* like her mother.

One day, the two sisters were brought together in the office for a family therapy session. The doctor questioned the lawyer and asked her how she felt about alcohol and why she was not experiencing the same difficulties as her sister. She replied that she had suffered so much from the difficult conditions of their childhood and from seeing their mother get into such a state. She had sworn to herself, on the one hand, that it would never happen to her, and on the other hand, that she would always help people with this problem as much as possible.

Responsibility is indeed a decision that one makes and a personal attitude, it is a state of mind that has nothing to do with circumstances.

Road accidents are also an area where we encounter this phenomenon. Very often bad weather, an oil puddle, or a misplaced tree seem to us much more harmful— this is not necessarily the case to others— than our own actions at the wheel.

If we want to gain confidence, we must make our own decisions whenever possible. Others have the right to their opinion— which is as respectable as ours— but it belongs to them.

> **Key points of the chapter:**
>
> ☑ A sense of responsibility is the key to freedom.
> ☑ It generates a powerful sense of autonomy, which is the hallmark of maturity.
> ☑ To be irresponsible is to wallow in the role of the victim.
> ☑ Victims do not win, they lose.
> ☑ We are responsible for everything, including our lives.
> ☑ Responsibility is a choice and a state of mind.

CHAPTER 10
THE FREQUENTATIONS

"You get credit for being with those who have it"

Jean-Baptiste Blanchard

Apart from family relationships that we don't choose, we hang out with people for reasons of affinity or common tastes, and those who spend a lot of time together often end up looking alike, literally and figuratively.

It is wise to look at our loved ones to get an idea of who we are, and to understand how others may look at us. "We're essentially an average of the five people we spend the most time with," says a common-sense popular saying.

This applies to all areas. There is a high probability that our attitudes, occupations, standards of living, and many other elements are the same, even down to our salary.

In November 2008, I had a serious motorcycle accident in Paris. I woke up the next day in the hospital with nineteen fractures. I underwent multiple operations and didn't go home until a month later. At home, I had to spend ten months in bed, three of them without being able to get up or move around much. My world had changed overnight. The only things I could do were read or watch television.

When I was able to start moving again and eventually go out almost a year later, I got into the habit of going to lunch at my gym. I found myself getting on well with a certain type of person and getting to know them quite naturally. Logically, like myself, they were living in slow motion. In fact, we didn't partake in a lot of activities and often stayed at home dividing our time between our books and our screens. We would spend hours at the club's bar chatting. We would remake the world; we would talk about the movie or the TV show from the day before. In short, I had spontaneously found the rhythm that suited me at that time, and I had surrounded myself with people in my own image. Of course, I am not making a qualitative judgment about their character, I am only referring to the way they chose to occupy their days.

Very quickly, I became depressed, and to overcome it, a few months later I played tennis again like before and did my laps every day in the pool. I also found myself once again, as if by magic, surrounded by enterprising and active relationships. I was back in the weight room within a short time. I had put an picture in my mind of me being in great shape. I knew I would be back to my old self, except for a few beautiful scars. It was my only option.

It is essential to take great care in choosing the people we spend time with. We must make the effort to reach out to people who are big creators, and whose lifestyle appeals to us, it is indispensable.

Surrounding ourselves with high performers has a beneficial influence and encourages us to give the best of ourselves. We don't have to feel guilty about being selective. We must surround ourselves with the best, with enthusiasm, and without any complex.

If we are reading this book, it is because we have decided to evolve. We will therefore spend our time with people who correspond to our path.

If we become aware, today or tomorrow, that there are people in our environment with whom we have less in common, we should take it as a sign. There is no harm in meeting them a little less often, and for a little less time. It's not a question of ignoring them or passing judgment, but we must know what we want and where we want to go.

We have already seen that the ego stands guard to prevent us from evolving. It is not the only one. Around us, some people may do the same. Whether we are doubling our income, achieving success at a higher level, or accomplishing something at an exceptional level, we may instill jealousy in those around us; this is normal. Moreover, this limitation will come sometimes from those close to us, that's how it is. Our success will bring the inability to evolve of some to light and confuse them. Let's not worry about it. Let's not be disappointed and let's not blame them; it's human.

If we go to the beach and put a crab in a bucket, it will cling to the edge and escape. If we catch a second one, we won't have to worry anymore because they will prevent each other from escaping; as soon as one of them reaches the edge, the second one will cling to it and bring it down.

This applies in general as well as in specific areas. If you are a sales representative and wish to improve your sales, it would be wise to frequent successful sales representatives. The same goes for top athletes; if your goal is to run a marathon or win a golf tournament, you should be with the best in these disciplines.

Mentoring is a form of association between two people with the aim of encouraging the transmission of knowledge. Being mentored by a high-performing person is a pragmatic action wherein we aim to benefit from his or her knowledge, which can save us time by avoiding us having to do certain experiments for ourselves.

A few years ago, I read *What Science for Tomorrow* by Frank Hatem[1], the great French metaphysician. I liked his book so much that I sent him an e-mail to let him know how enthusiastic I was. Frank replied, and one thing led to another and we became close. I can't count the hours we spent at his house during which Frank shared his knowledge with me, and I'm thankful for the friendship we have today.

---

[1] (Édions Ganimed, 2002).

Frank is ahead of our time and his work on the origin of consciousness is the missing link. Unfortunately, but logically, Nobel Prizes are rarely awarded to those whose work threatens the comfort zone of the system and of science.

I have lost count of the hours we have spent at his home sharing his knowledge with me, and I am happy with the friendship we have today.

Frank also introduced me to Léon-Raoul, his father, who, in 1955, made major discoveries on the cause of the appearance of the universe. The day that my son and I had come to see Léon-Raoul, he demonstrated it to me in his living room with his original models. It was a magical moment.

As this book is about coaching, I also met Bob Proctor— the king of coaches— for the first time in Los Angeles in the lobby of a hotel where he was conducting one of his seminars. Bob taught me a lot, and without him, this book would not be the same. Today he is over 85 and he continues to pass his knowledge on to entire crowds in seminars, sometime speaking and standing for over eight hours a day.

This coach is an enigma to everyone who knows him. He, himself attributes his energy to his refusal to give in to comfort and his desire to evolve every day.

His wisdom is immense, and he is always happy to pass it on with kindness. We kept in touch and Bob later welcomed me to his home in Toronto during one of his "Matrix" events. Here, I shot a video sitting at his desk, in front of his library, in his television studio where he broadcasts his teaching to over one hundred and twenty countries.

These two fantastic encounters would never have taken place if I had not transformed my desires into action, that is, by taking the necessary steps. If we want to learn something and move forward in a field, we must be enterprising and surround ourselves with the best.

Sometimes I can't believe the tenor of some conversations in which people give or listen to the opinions of other people whose track record shows no valid results. Listening to someone's advice because they are present at that time or for emotional reasons of affinity is absurd.

Every day, single people give marriage advice to their couple friends, unemployed people give professional recommendations to entrepreneurs, unhealthy people give dietary or exercise advice to those around them; it's unbelievable!

Giving advice before you have achieved outstanding results is crazy.

For my part, I consider the advice I receive only if the people who give it to me have obtained the kind of results I am aiming for in the field in question. It is obvious that following the advice received will lead us to the same results as those who gave it to us.

We always come back to the essential notion of result; the result is fundamental, and it is even the only significant thing, insofar as it has been obtained without harming anyone.

Making recommendations for the simple pleasure of hearing oneself talk or to show off is a waste of everyone's time. In fact, it is in our best interest to give advice only to the extent that we have been asked for it, since those who give advice are rarely the ones who act.

And let's face it, so often people ask for an opinion just because they need approval and lack confidence. They already know deep down inside what they're going to do anyway.

Of course, the same applies to our hobbies and occupations which deserve to be selected with the utmost care. Reading a book by Schopenhauer or watching a dumb reality show will not have the same effect.

The way of talking to yourself and to others is also to be studied when you want to improve your self-image. Certain formulas and words that we use every day prove to be counterproductive. There are so many that it is impossible to list them all, but here are one or two to understand the principle. Expressions such as: "I'm not going to make it," "It's impossible," "It's unfair," and, "It sucks," are good examples. It is better to say, "I will," rather than, "I must," or, "I have to". Words like "challenge" or "obstacle" are better than "problem". With a little common sense, we can find others.

Let's also talk about the "super-victims" who spend their time talking about their difficulties or their illnesses, and who transform their entourage into "offices for listening to laments". We have all noticed how these people navigate from one concern to another, taking pleasure in recounting them. Sometimes you will even see them use very technical terms.

It is understandable that these people have conducted research to identify and understand their ills. This is one way they have found to get attention. but it is not doing them a favor to give it to them. Feeling sorry for them will not get them out of the trap in which they have locked themselves. It is better for them if we help them regain their self-confidence by explaining to them that we become the equivalent of the thoughts we entertain.

Their situation is sad, we can help them get out of it. But be careful. In cases where the person identifies with his or her own behavior, it is best to be diplomatic. Reflecting on certain attitudes can hurt those who resort to victimization, because they have difficulty differentiating between their attitudes and their person.

Such a posture is horribly damaging, and the subconscious ravages can be enormous. In my immediate surroundings, I come across fully able-bodied people who use handicapped cards to be able to park more easily. I'm not even talking about the problems that their behavior creates for truly disabled people who can't find space. Can we even imagine the effect of such acts on their own self-esteem?

Lies are always counterproductive and destructive to the deepest image of those who commit them but pretending to be a disabled person when you are able-bodied is really distressing, even if they don't realize it. We all do for the best depending on our level of awareness.

Turning to weakness is never an option if one is aiming for confidence and the achievement of one's goals. And we must also help those who have not understood this.

Key points of the chapter:

- ☑ Those who act alike come together.
- ☑ Let's surround ourselves with people who win in all areas.
- ☑ The praise of weakness is a losing hand.
- ☑ Success is contagious.
- ☑ Coaching is an excellent way to progress.
- ☑ Let's only take the advice of those who have achieved outstanding results.

CHAPTER 11
TAKING ACTION

"Action is the fundamental key to success"

Pablo Picasso

The capacities of human beings seem endless, and no one today can assess their limits. Whether they are physical, through sports performances, or mental, as can be seen in every invention, they seem to always go further and further. This is to believe in the existence of a kind of collective dynamic, in view of the acceleration of the technical developments of the 20th century or the electronic developments of the last thirty years.

We know we all have the same brain, but we don't all act the same way. The great discoveries are man-made, and I wonder if we realize today what it meant, for example, to declare five hundred years ago that the Earth was round and that it revolved around the Sun. Not only did you have to be damn sharp, intellectually speaking, but you had to have a self-image of monumental strength. The Copernicans, the Newtons, the Galileo's and all the others had the whole planet against them when they revealed their discoveries.

They were hated by most of the people who wanted to burn them alive... Sailors at that time feared that they would venture too far and fall into the void when they reached the end of the Earth. Both Benz and the Wright brothers conducted their respective automotive and aviation experiments in secret, because people made fun of them and threw stones at them in the street— this was less than a hundred and fifty years ago. They all had a dream, a vision, and a concrete thinking, which allowed us to be where we are today.

To think that nowadays we continue to point fingers at all those who do not submit to the dictates of conformity is to despair of everything. Earl Nightingale, one of the pioneers of personal development in the 50s, used to say that the opposite of courage is not cowardice but conformism, and that to succeed in life, you just must do the exact opposite of what most people do.

We talked a lot about theory in the first part of this book, a necessary step to understanding the foundations of self-confidence and a strong self-image, in order to create the required state of mind. To this state of mind, we must of course add *action*. One might be tempted to say that a superior self-image without action would take us nowhere, but this would not be entirely true. With a strong image, it would be impossible not to act.

We have seen that feelings of gratitude and responsibility are powerful stimulants, and we will now address their opposite— the most powerful brake— which is *fear*. When we do not act, fear is often the main cause of our inaction.

112

Fear is a state of mind, and for things to come true in our lives, we must learn to ruthlessly eliminate this obstacle.

To achieve this, it is necessary to identify it as soon as it appears and face it. It is indeed often subconscious, has many faces and is skillfully hidden under many other feelings such as doubt, uncertainty, indecision, anxiety, etc.

When we can't make up our minds and when we doubt or worry, it reveals that something is scaring us. Many things stem from fear in a direct or indirect way. Fear has a paralyzing power like no other, and the expression, "scared to death," is not a coincidence. Fear freezes us and brings us to a standstill.

Habits— which lead to a refusal to evolve— also originate in the fear of the unknown.

When we find ourselves in the grip of fear, we are invaded by it and see nothing else. No other emotion is so destructive.

The part of the brain that reacts to fear is the part that manages the survival instinct. It is a primitive part, also called the reptilian brain. It is located at the back base, opposite— as if by chance— to the part that governs thought. We will go into this in more detail soon.

When the mechanisms of fear are activated, reflexes replace all forms of reflection. A kind of primitive egotism takes control of the maneuver, and woe betides anyone who stands in the way of someone under the control of fear. This explains why, in the event of a health crisis for example, some people fill their shopping cart with enough packages of toilet paper to last several months, without the slightest concern for the needs of others. More tragically, and for the same reasons, in fires, some people jostle others and push them out of the way in order to escape more quickly.

Submission to authority also occurs under the effect of fear, where all forms of autonomy are annihilated. Dictators know this and use it as much as they can. People all over the world submit more easily to their leaders if they are under the influence of fear, oftentimes in the face of great catastrophes such as wars, crises, famines, and other pandemics.

Machiavelli said, "He who controls people's fear becomes the master of their souls". If this maxim was inlaid as a subtitle on the news (always bad), the world would not be the same.

No one can boast of not having encountered fear in one form or another, mild or acute, whether it is fear of poverty, illness, suffering, failure, loss of a loved one, criticism, or judgment of others or death of course.

Fear is hidden everywhere, even in the most trivial acts. Why do many people run out and buy the latest "fashionable" clothes? Isn't this a way of submitting to the judgment of others for fear of appearing out-of-date? Believe me, it is indeed the fear in all its forms which hides behind many behaviors and it never brings anything good, neither for its victim, nor for its entourage.

It is very often under fear's control that individuals seek to control the actions of others. We have never seen a fulfilled person seeking to selfishly lead others.

Fear is eliminated through knowledge and reason. The more we study, the more we reason, and the more we realize that fear is, in fact, only an illusion. It is also enough to know that fear diminishes each time we cross its barriers and confront it. Let's call it the repetition of acts of courage, with a snowball effect.

Let's hunt fear down and eliminate it, rather than submit to it. Let's even go so far as to strike it from our vocabulary by deleting expressions such as, "I'm afraid of," which prove to be infinitely less diminishing than they seem.

To conclude on this subject, let us note that Napoleon Hill, the father of success analysts, wrote a book of several hundred pages solely on fear. This book was so innovative and revolutionary that his family did not agree to publish it until seventy years after it was written, conscious of the "paving stone in the pond of conformism" that this book would represent. The title of the book, *Outwitting the Devil*,[1] clearly tells us about the author's idea of fear and the fact that it had to be mastered for us to evolve.

We must therefore act without wavering when we have determined our priorities, whether we feel ready or not. We will evolve and adapt along the way.

---

[1] *Outwitting the devil. The Secret of Freedom and Success* (Aska editions, 2013).

This motivation that pushes us to act is related to the intensity of the desire that drives us. Paradoxically, it can draw its source from the consequences of a suffering or an important emotional shock.

This is why it is sometimes easier to rise from a dramatic condition than from a simply mediocre one. The more uncomfortable our situation is, the more motivated we will be to act. It's a bit like the bottom of the pool, which we push against to rise faster.

Indeed, the greatest human achievements have almost always come about as a result of failures. This proves that, no matter what situation we find ourselves in, there is a high probability of a major improvement.

Sara Blakely is an excellent example of someone who symbolizes this ideology. Sara dreamed of a bright future. She experienced rejection, failure and remained in a kind of in-between indecision for seven years before taking action.

Sara had always wanted to be a lawyer. Her father practiced the profession himself, which created a favorable environment for her. After her studies, she registered for the bar exam so that she could begin her training, but she failed. Her marks were not good enough. She decided to re-register the following year and she studied hard to get different marks. She succeeded, but not in the way she had hoped. Her average was lower than it was the previous year.

She gave up and applied for a summer job at Disneyland, following the recommendation of a friend. She had to wear the Goofy costume and walk the park's pathways to entertain the children. But once again she failed; her measurements didn't match the size of the costume— no less frustrating for her than her grades. She also failed in her second choice— the Chip and Dale costumes— and had to settle for putting people on a merry-go-round dressed in a silver polyester cosmonaut costume for several hours a day in the California summer sun.

Following this experience, Sara worked a series of odd jobs in order to stay active and earn a living. One day, she joined a company that sold fax machines, with the mission of canvassing individuals at home to sell her merchandise. It wasn't easy, because nine times out of ten, she would get the door slammed in her face, not to mention many people's refusal to open the door for her at all. In addition, her inventory was being stolen from her van about once a week, and she was reprimanded by her employer. She held this job for seven years.

She would later state that she never stopped thinking, all that time, that one day she would start her own business, adding that the positive thing she had gained from those years was that she had become totally insensitive to rejection. This gave her great strength.

Sara was a coquettish young woman, and the fact that the elastic of her underwear was visible through her pants had always bothered her. One day, she took a pair of tights, cut off the feet and put them under her pants. She was very satisfied with the result, both in terms of comfort and aesthetics. She thought she had found her business. She resigned and alone, without telling anyone, meticulously prepared and perfected her project.

The path was strewn with obstacles. Sara had only $5,000 to get started, but she knew what she wanted, and her life had become exciting. Eventually, her business got off to a great start and grew remarkably. All her products can now be found under the name *Spanx*, both on the internet and in many stores.

Sara was the first female, self-made billionaire by the age of forty. Today her foundation helps many children around the world and assists many women who are also aspiring entrepreneurs.

Key points of the chapter:

- ☑ The capacities of the human being are virtually without limits.
- ☑ The only limits are in the brain.
- ☑ Fear is at the root of all negative feelings.
- ☑ It is through knowledge that we can break down our internal barriers.
- ☑ The opposite of courage is conformism.
- ☑ Once our objectives are defined, we must act and move forward.
- ☑ It is only after the first step that the road takes shape.

CHAPTER 12
LEARNING

"To know and not to do is not to know."

Leo Buscaglia

A few years ago, the director of a large insurance company asked a consultant to intervene in his company with its five hundred salespeople to make them more efficient.

The consultant arrived just as the company was about to hold a major year-end meeting, during which several of the salespeople gave speeches on stage, including the company's number one salesman, John. He received the honors and spoke for over an hour in a large hotel reception hall.

The consultant began his work the next day in the company, where he circulated for several days. He questioned the employees, tried to understand how they worked and analyzed the figures. The day he came face-to-face with John, the number one salesman, he learned that the other salesmen in the company had never questioned him to try to understand how he had managed to achieve such results in the five years he had been working at the company.

Although there is *nothing* more logical for people spending the whole day with someone who achieves the results you are aiming for, to ask them how they do it, no one has ever done it before. The thought had simply never occurred to anyone. Not one employee had ever spent even a minute of their time on it.

The consultant was not surprised. What was going through the minds of the other vendors was that they thought John was kind of an alien with mysterious abilities. In their eyes, he was different from them. Their self-image and ego had blocked any possibility of evolution in them. They didn't allow themselves to get better results, and the case was closed.

John himself felt frustrated; he would have loved to have had someone take an interest in his work methods, and he would have been happy to help his colleagues. He was succeeding, and, like anyone who really wins, he was eager to help others. People with a finished mind are not in competition but in creation, as we now know. They seek to create, for themselves and for others.

The ultimate outcome for John would have been to raise the whole level of his company. All his colleagues would have had to have done was know their potential, but they were limited by the false image they had of themselves. They lacked faith and the knowledge of the mechanisms of success.

The best remedy against limitations is, indeed, knowledge. Let us recall; the more we study, the more we become free and aware.

It is extremely beneficial to try and study every day so that it becomes a habit. It is not necessary to work for a long time. Reading a paragraph may even be enough. At the very least, it will always be beneficial. Many people find daily study necessary; it is as important for some as regular exercise.

We also know that we can develop new neurons throughout our lives; contrary to what was believed for a long time. We knew it was possible to maintain our neurons by working them— just like a muscle— but now we know we can create new ones, regardless of our age.

To do this, we must get our brain to work in a new way; by surprising it. Neurons are created out of necessity, so that we can adapt to new situations.

The appearance of new neurons occurs not only when we learn new things, but also when we perform new actions. We thus understand that by living routinely, we are setting the stage for intellectual regression and even cellular degeneration.

It is important to distinguish between learning and storing information, because they are two very different things. Contrary to what many people think, learning does not only mean accumulating new knowledge. Learning means *adopting a new behavior.*

For this to happen, you must first experiment with new behaviors, and adjust them based on feedback. If we have not acquired new habits or acquired and put into practice new know-how, we have learned nothing. We have informed ourselves, which is fine, but it's not the same thing.

If we read a book about flying or surfing, we have stored up information on these subjects. In no case have we learned how to fly a plane or how to surf. In order to achieve this, we will also have to combine theory with practice.

We can read thousands of pages on psychology, personal development, or human functioning without changing anything in our existence.

Another way to learn is through demonstration and repetition. The tennis teacher begins by performing the movement in front of the student who then reproduces and repeats it hundreds of times. These repetitions make the practice more effective and make it a habit. The same applies to education; parents must know that children do what their parents *do*, not what they *tell them* to do.

To think that reading a book alone will change your results is pure utopia. That's why this one is accompanied by a program in the second part. On the other hand, it can be a trigger or a first step.

This in no way calls into question the benefits of cultivation, nor the value that a cultivated person has acquired, but that is not the purpose of this program. Reading is, of course, an exceptional leisure activity. The knowledge contained in books is the key to wisdom. An intelligentsia has passed on the fruit of reflections from generation to generation for thousands of years. The most brilliant people have worked and reflected all their lives on all subjects and made the fruit of their work available to us. Their path has not only been intellectual, but also material, and they also give us information about their lives. They give us valuable advice and save us from having to take certain steps on our own.

The entire school system, which is undergoing very profound changes, is based on the principle of information storage. The secret for the student is to recall, on the day of the exam, the elements of information that have been transmitted to them beforehand. If they succeed in doing so, they will complete their studies brilliantly and pass their exams with honors.

This is not a criticism of the school or of the curriculum, which are essential— I, myself, monitor my children's studies with great enthusiasm, because their success in this area is of paramount importance.

Yet it is difficult not to be challenged by the number of over-educated people who point to unemployment, and the number of people who have not received formal education and yet find themselves at the head of multinational corporations or inventing things that change the world.

The reason for this, which is the subject of this book, is quite simple: the brain (where knowledge is stored) is under the control of self-image. If our programming is successful, then things are in good order. If not, we have every interest in modifying it in-depth. The effort alone is not enough, in the long run.

The philosophy of success, which constitutes the first theoretical part of this book, can be defined in one word: *evolution*. It comes to us after a long millennial transmission line. It entered its modern version about a hundred years ago, through Andrew Carnegie, who was a major pivot in the updating of this teaching.

Andrew Carnegie was born in Scotland in 1835 to a working-class family who emigrated to the United States when he was thirteen years old. In his youth, he had a passion for reading and spent all his free time in the libraries near his home.

Later, he worked in the steel mill and his specialty was making railway rails. His professional success was as colossal as it was unprecedented.

Andrew Carnegie was a good and generous man. He made it a point of honor to treat his workers well, which was unusual at the time. He contributed to the cultural development of hundreds of millions of people by building libraries, theaters, institutes, and museums, which he donated to cities around the world.

He created pension funds for teachers to continue to teach, as well as the Carnegie Endowment for World Peace, and many other charitable endeavors. Today, there are countless public buildings around the world bearing his name.

After the Revolution, France had built a very important library in Reims, which housed many works of international renown. During the First World War, it was destroyed, and, just like the city, it was devastated. Thanks to the generosity of the Carnegie Foundation, it was rebuilt in 1920. If we want to go there today, it's quite simple: the Carnegie Library, located at 2 place Carnegie in Reims.

When he was sixty-six years old, Carnegie became the fourth or fifth richest man of all time. From that day on, he stopped working and only redistributed his assets, without any personal expenses. He said that to disappear with money was a disgrace and he managed to give almost all his fortune to good causes before he died.

This man was one of the greatest benefactors in history. He helped to spread and pass on knowledge from generation to generation.

Key points of the chapter:

- ☑ Knowledge is a remedy for overcoming one's limits.
- ☑ Neurons maintain and grow themselves every day.
- ☑ Learning does not mean storing information.
- ☑ To learn is to acquire a new know-how.
- ☑ Learning is synonymous with progress.
- ☑ The ultimate outcome of evolution is to help others evolve.

CHAPTER 13
FORGET LOGIC

"Logic is the last refuge of the unima-
ginative"

Oscar Wilde

With this chapter, we end the first part of this book in which we have listed all the ingredients that make up the recipe for success.

So far, we have reasoned from our current condition, and now we want to go further. The logic that has guided us until now obviously cannot take us there, even if we are beginning to see things in a new light.

As we have seen in the foreword, it is impossible to solve a problem with the same method of thinking that generated the problem. We're going to have to forget about our logic and stop believing that it necessarily guides us to success.

When we are sick, we go to the doctor. A man whose job it is to care for people gets his income if people get sick, and we find that logical. In traditional Chinese medicine, on the contrary, the village doctor is paid according to the villager's state of health; the less sick they get, the better his income.

Medicine is then synonymous with good health. It is obviously not medicine or doctors who are responsible for this.

There are a considerable number of counter-intuitive things in life— especially in the area of success and achievement, —that make us "intuitively" do that which we definitely should not. Some things are deceptive, and our actions take us away from the desired result, in good faith.

For the same reason, we refrain from doing what we should do, mistakenly believing that it will bring us a negative result.

In financial matters, this sentiment is also particularly true. Statistics show that less than 3% of the population achieves a high level of income from their investments. Most people who own shares with rising prices sell them and keep those with declining prices, however, savvy traders do exactly the opposite: they keep shares that rise and sell them as they decline.

We sometimes act a bit like moths attracted by the light of a light bulb, only to find themselves trapped in a place that will prove fatal to them. Whether they turn tirelessly around the light bulb or bump into the closed windowpane a thousand times, they repeat the same gesture until they die. Often, they even disregard the door that is open a few meters away.

The moral of the story is that doing more of something that is wrong is obviously not the solution. Sometimes it is enough to do things differently, and with infinitely less effort.

Every day, people get robbed at the "three card trick". It has been going on for a thousand years, and we can conservatively estimate that hundreds of millions of people have been fleeced because they have followed "blindly" (if I may say so...) their visual logic.

Not everyone is familiar with the principle of counter steering on a two-wheeler. When you are on a motorcycle, if you push the left handlebar forward without tilting the bike, it will go left and not right as expected. It's absurd, but that's the way it is. I've talked to perfectly intelligent people who refused to believe me until they checked it out on the internet. I assured them of the phenomenon, but there was nothing I could do to prove it. Anyone with a motorcycle or scooter can check it.

Another example. A few years ago, I had two friends with whom I used to go out a lot. One was named Alexis and the other Jérôme. The first was single— and he intended to stay single— and the second was also single but spent most of his days trying to get out of that state. Alexis was surrounded by suitors, while Jérôme never got beyond the friendship stage with the girls he met. He was relegated forever to the *friend zone*.

Wherever Alexis showed up, it was always more or less the same thing. He would arrange to be in the immediate vicinity of the prettiest girl in the place while royally ignoring her, and he would start the conversation with the people around him.

A little later, he would approach the young woman to exchange, for the first time, a few sentences. Looking her in the eye, he would make a remark about the shape of her lips or tell her that he could see her with her hair up or something like that. This mini conversation lasted five minutes, and then he would leave saying, most naturally, that he was going back to his friends and that they would both see each other later. The next time we went out, he and the young woman would always arrive together.

Jérôme, for his part, did not have the same attitude in the evening. When he liked a woman, he would devour her with his eyes without daring to speak to her. Once the ice was broken, usually by a third person, he would only address her with a sweet voice and put her under terrible pressure. From that moment on, we, his friends, no longer existed to him. Sometimes he would ask the young woman if he could buy her a drink, invite her to dinner somewhere else, or go to the movies the following weekend, sometimes all in one sentence. If the young woman had asked him to get on his knees, he would not have hesitated for a second. We also knew that, several times a day, he was texting and calling the unhappy gals who were kind enough to give him their cell phone numbers.

We tried to reason with him more than fifty times to no avail. He didn't understand that Alexis' success came from remaining relaxed while his, in his own words, "consideration and kindness," made him unsuccessful. That Alexis was cool and stress-free didn't occur to him either. Neither that, nor the fact that a woman could be attracted to a man who looked good in his sneakers rather than someone whose *self-image* had remained at the level of his socks. By putting his "promises" on such a pedestal, he implicitly acknowledged that he did not feel up to the task. He thought he could convince us of his views; however, he was only demonstrating that he did not believe in himself.

Sometimes Jérôme would be bitter and say, "That's shameful! You don't care, whereas I'm super nice". Rather than telling him for the umpteenth time that it wasn't that Alexis, "didn't care," instead, he was just cool, we would tease him a little and say, "You're right. The little difference that makes the difference is indifference". It wasn't necessarily a high-flying thought, but we were teenagers. These are still great memories today.

He was looking for a girlfriend and was needy and unsuccessful. The one who was more distant was courted. This is another example of a counter-intuitive phenomenon. One more story to blame on low self-image.

The moral of this story is that we will have to follow and do what is recommended in the second part of this book, even if our logic tries to dissuade us from doing so.

This is obviously true in the other direction. How many times have I seen women push away men who were at their feet in legions, when their friends would have given everything to be in their place? There's nothing unfair about that.

While this may seem illogical to some, it is very normal. We know that our thoughts create our reality. Being needy is opposite of "having" mindset.

Forgetting the reason that seeks to hold us back or that pushes us to play it safe is a habit that we must cultivate.

Sandy, the young woman we talked about with a sense of gratitude, had a dream. She wanted to buy a beautiful home on an island off the West coast of Washington State. As she knew the mechanics of success, she began to leaf through the catalog of the most prestigious real estate agency in the area. She didn't care about the rates and started dreaming about a beautiful property overlooking a lake. When she read the price, it did not correspond at all to the amount she had decided to invest in this purchase.

She told Bob her partner, and he challenged her to do something to motivate her: Sandy was to send a letter to her parents and her entire family inviting them to celebrate Christmas in this house a few months later. She did as such, however, not without apprehension. After that, her brain started to work in a certain way; it searched for solutions. Sandy adapted her behavior to her dream, and she managed to create professional opportunities for herself. She had a goal and set out towards it. She was able to celebrate the holiday season in her beautiful home surrounded by her entire family, and the Christmas turkey was eaten by the lake.

Let's talk about Phil Goldfine. A successful Hollywood film producer who has already won an Emmy and an Oscar. He decided last year to add a Tony Award to his trophy collection, by adapting the film *Tootsie* for the theater. During a big evening where there were hundreds of people packed in a room, he opened to Bob also one of his friends who was organizing the event. Bob asked the room to be quiet. Then he invited Phil to stand on his chair and give the acceptance speech that he would give six months later when he would actually receive the award. Phil was used to the podium and he did it. He found the words to deliver his speech without difficulty.

He received his Tony shortly thereafter.

I guarantee you that this is not a fable or a beautiful story that is told to make you dream. As amazing as it is, it is very real. I was there that night and I remember Phil talking, standing in his chair. I can't hide from you that I was really looking forward to the results of the Tony's in the time that followed.

What Sandy and Phil did was totally illogical, but this is the result. They burned their vessels and they succeeded.

This seems interesting to me and it would be too easy for me to talk about coincidence. Voltaire said that this word was invented to designate something that our intelligence could not explain. Finding themselves in a position they had voluntarily put themselves in, Sandy and Phil's respective attitudes certainly changed to allow them to achieve their goals. Their levers were their very strong emotions. Sending an invitation to your family to a place you don't yet own or giving an acceptance speech at a Hollywood party before you have received an award must have stirred them up quite a bit.

We have seen that many seemingly incomprehensible things can be explained by the fact that human acts more according to his emotions than his reason.

We have gone over it, but let's go a little deeper into this point: the human brain has developed gradually, over the course of its evolution, in three parts. The primitive or physical part at the back base, the emotional part at the center, and finally the intellectual— or, rational— part at the top and front. To put it simply, the primitive— or reptilian— part deals mainly with survival and reproduction; the emotional— or mammalian— part deals mainly with emotions; and the intellectual— or neocortex— part deals with reason. This is why we sometimes feel an inner tear when we are faced with a dilemma. In fact, it is because all three parts of our brain are in conflict.

What is important to know is that reason does not carry much weight, and is quickly swept away when the primitive brain, which reacts to fear, or the emotional brain, which reacts to emotions, are called upon.

*

We have now completed the first part of this book and will move on to the practical stage in the following chapters, as the exercises are presented.

These are particularly powerful and will enable us to break the chain of circumstances and choose our future.

They must be done without considering limiting thoughts that might arise; we have often talked about our deep defense mechanisms that push back change.

Whether you find these exercises illogical, unusual, or stupid, that's not the point. They are extremely effective in improving your life, making you more productive, and making you happier. Remember all the examples at the beginning of this chapter of those situations where we stray, in good faith, from our goals and think we are getting closer to them.

Firstly, we will objectively and accurately assess our beliefs. Then we will define our objectives, both in terms of behaviors and results. Then we will change our beliefs and rebuild our image based on our own decisions.

I envy you today as you begin this exciting and rewarding journey. Trust me and let me be your guide.

Key points of the chapter:

- ☑ We form our logic according to where we are today.
- ☑ It is impossible for us to evolve maintaining our current logic.
- ☑ Many things are counterintuitive and make us commit counterproductive actions.
- ☑ Many other things, which we don't do, would help us to succeed.
- ☑ The second part of this book offers an exhilarating journey.
- ☑ Let yourself be guided and you will be happy.

Part Two
The program

CHAPTER 14
BALANCE SHEET

"Know yourself"
Socrates

We now know that we all have a profound image of ourselves, which is linked to our level of confidence, and which directly controls our behaviors and, indirectly, our results.

Now let's get to work with the first exercise. In the next chapter, we will write our self-portrait and learn how to use it according to a precise method to deeply impact our unconscious mechanisms. Notable progress and results will follow almost immediately.

So, the first thing to do is to take stock of who we think we are to-date. We will carry out this personal inventory in a methodical way in all areas of our existence. It is likely that this first exercise will take several days. Work seriously and keep your enthusiasm.

When we are looking for a job, we send a CV to a future employer in order to define ourselves and describe our career path. In the case of dating sites, we introduce ourselves by writing a profile of ourselves so that others can get a picture of us.

We will now do much the same, following a precise methodology. Even if you are not used to using your time for self-reflection, especially in writing, it is nevertheless a highly beneficial exercise and very fun.

Writing does not impact our unconscious in the same way as speech, because the mechanisms and neurons used are different. The result is, in fact, much deeper. Thats why, when faced with an important decision to make, many people turn to pen and paper. It is sometimes very useful, when faced with a difficulty, to write down all the elements of a problem. This helps to clarify thinking and, by putting it in order, allows the brain to be more efficient. The movement of the pen on paper, in correlation with the thought, acts in a certain way on the brain. This is not the same as simple reflection.

It is also important to know that other connections are used when we watch a video or listen to a recording. For my part, when I want to permanently store new information— taking a course or learning a new language, for example— I study in all four ways: reading, writing, listening to recordings, and watching videos on the subject. I've been doing this for years. I'm besieging my brain from all sides. It's extremely effective.

You will now need a quiet room, a piece of paper, and a pen. You are going to reflect on several aspects of your life. A note for the die-hard computer-users: the exercise will be less beneficial with a computer keyboard, but it will still be quite feasible and profitable.

Start by writing a detailed description of yourself. Only you will read what you are going to write, so don't fool yourself, and be as honest as possible for your own sake. Write down your qualities as well as your shortcomings, because in the next chapter you will work on both by reinforcing your strengths and reviewing your weaknesses. Everything you will write is not what you *are*, but rather what you *believe* you are. It is going to be about your actual *perception*.

In order to make this self-portrait complete, here are a few guidelines, but, obviously, you are completely free: The main thing is to remain enthusiastic and to conform to my model as much as possible. The exercise will be beneficial no matter how you do it, but the more precise you are, and the more elements you will address, the more effective it will be. Anything can be improved by working on it.

Here are the elements to be addressed:

1. Your appearance.
2. Your character, your behavior, and your mind.
3. Your hygiene, your well-being, your physical condition.
4. Your Relationship with others.

5. Your job.

6. The state of your finances.

These different aspects will be more than enough to describe you.

So, grab some writing materials and a few sheets of paper and let's get started.

Write, "My Balance Sheet," or an equivalent phrase at the top of the paper and begin to address the points above. Mention a few adjectives to define your appearance, the way you dress, your character, your behaviors, your activities, the quality of your social relationships, your work, etc.

Below, to guide you, I have presented the assessment of two people who did this exercise (Franck and Caroline). You will work using the same method. You will see that they were honest and were not afraid to expose their perceived weaknesses. These two examples will help you take stock by making your own choices of adjectives and letting your instincts guide you. The only rule of thumb is to define yourself as much as possible in the six departments listed above. Make sure to focus on the elements that are particularly important to you— both positive and negative— and mark each with a + or - sign, respectively.

Don't be afraid of not knowing what to write, just get started. You will find, by doing this very personal exercise, that your unconscious itself will help you, that inspiration will come progressively, and that ideas will germinate naturally in your brain.

Writers are familiar with this mechanism: when they write a book, they sit down in front of a blank sheet of paper and ideas begin to flow in on their own.

Assessment of Franck, a 30-year-old man

APPEARENCE	CHARACTER, MENTAL
5'9" - 30 years	Lack of trust (-)
Weight problem (too big) (-)	Boasting (-)
Smiling face (+)	Intelligent (+)
Sympathetic face (+)	Indelicate (-)
Clothing often neglected (-)	Cultivated (+)
Clean (+)	Undisciplined (-)
	Speaks 4 languages (+)
	Curious (+)
	Sporty (+)
	Tendency to be egocentric (-)

RELATIONS	JOB
Entrepreneurial (+)	Income $ 4,000
Dynamic (+)	Restaurant manager (+)
Lots of friends (+)	Loves my work (+)
Very few close friends (-)	Often changes jobs (-)
Sometimes Intolerant (-)	Salary that does not change (-)
Unreliable (-)	

FINANCE	FITNESS, HOBBIES
Bank loans (-)	Robust (+)
No savings (-)	Never sick (+)
Borrowed from my friends (-)	Sports (+) (Volleyball, Football, Tennis)

Assessment of Caroline, a 50-year-old woman

APPEARANCE	CHARACTER, MENTAL
5'9" - 50 years old	Reserved (+/-)
Slim (+)	Conscientious (+)
Clean (+)	Distant/removed from socializing (-)
Likes to get dressed (+)	Honest (+)
I don't think I'm pretty enough (-)	Skeptical (-)
People find me bland (-)	Reliable (+)
	Sporty (+)
	Serious (+)
	Yoga (+)

RELATIONS	JOB
Gentile (+)	Photographer (+)
Some good friends (+)	Meticulous (+)
Gets out infrequently (-)	Passionate (+)
	Artistic (+)
	Gifted (+)
	Generous (+)

FINANCE	FITNESS, HOBBIES
Apartment & country house (+)	Fragile (-)
Investments (+)	Yoga (+)
Art photo collection (+)	Gym (+)
Vacations, few trips (-)	Swimming (+)
Good salary (+)	

We could say, by schematizing a little, that we have on one side Franck and his slightly indelicate attitude, and on the other Caroline and her discretion.

Franck is a very intelligent, cultured, and resourceful man. He is robust and sporty. His deep lack of confidence— which he acknowledges— limits and embarrasses him on a daily basis. He hides it behind a sometimes boastful and somewhat brutal facade, and he also lacks tolerance in some cases. This explains the paradox between his dynamic and smiling side of the man who likes to party, and his difficulties in certain situations or with a certain style of people. His professional results are not up to par with his faculties due to a lack of discipline.

Caroline lacks self-confidence for no reason, as is always the case; when you know the human potential, it is absurd that anyone can lack confidence. Caroline, contrary to Franck, is ultra-performing in her work, with excellent results. In her private life, she is reserved, and she would also like to grow by having more confidence in herself and in her qualities, and to approach others more often.

Take these two descriptions only for what they are for you: simple examples to understand how to write your own balance sheet. Now it's up to you to do yours.

This exercise will certainly allow you to get a better understanding of yourself if you do it seriously, by investing the necessary time and thought. You must persevere and work a little bit every day on this program. You will find that things will start to move very quickly. This is usually the case when you start working on yourself in depth. Observe yourself in the hours and days ahead, as you will likely see a positive effect on your mood or feel lighter or more confident in certain areas.

The next step now is to link these adjectives together, using sentences, and to write a portrait that forms a short story. Half a page to one full page is an appropriate length in this case. Again, you can refer to the portraits of Frank and Caroline to draw your own.

Self-portrait of Franck

My name is Franck X[1] . I'm single and I'm 5'9" tall. I have a smiling face, I have short, brown hair. I am a clean person and I

---

[1] Indicate your last name well: it is important, because it is a way to assert yourself; to affirm your own personality.

148

dress casually without worrying too much about my outfit. I find myself too fat.

I like meeting people, but I don't hang out with "uptight" people because I don't get along with them and I don't like their ways. I am intelligent, and curious about everything. Thus, I like to read, and I am cultured. This natural curiosity has allowed me to learn and speak four languages, which makes my life much easier when I travel abroad. I am active and I play many sports; mainly tennis.

I'm a pretty straightforward person and I don't mind telling people, frankly, what I think. I don't like to come across as passive. The pleasures of life are important to me, and I like to party with my friends over a good bottle or a good cigar.

I prefer casual acquaintances to close friends because I'm always on the move.

I work in catering and I like it. My salary is $4,000 a month. I would like to earn more, but I change jobs often because I like to do what I want, and I find it difficult to obey directions that I don't always understand.

This honest portrait fits perfectly with Franck's first assessment of himself.

Self-portrait of Caroline

My name is Caroline Y, I am 5'75" tall and I am slim. I don't think I'm pretty enough. I attach a lot of importance to my outfit, I'm hygienic, and I like to dress in a rather unremarkable way so as not to be noticed. Sometimes, people comment that they consider my wardrobe too plain.

I am married to Éric who cares for me, and I have two beautiful children, Karen and Brian, whom I love.

I am a sincere, honest, and very conscientious person; I know that people can count on me. I sometimes have difficulty reaching out to others because I am a bit reserved and skeptical, due to certain unfortunate experiences in previous friendships. I would like to meet more people and go out more often with friends. People who know me generally find me very pleasant. I have two very good friends that I love to go out with. I have found my equilibrium this way.

I work out and I love practicing yoga every day because I have noticed that it stabilizes me and makes me feel more confident.

I'm a photographer and I love my job; it's my passion. I have always loved everything related to art. I work a lot and people offer me new interesting work every day.

Thanks to this, I am proud to earn a good living and I was able to offer my family a beautiful country house. I also give money to several charities.

We travel a little, but we must be careful, because my health is often a concern.

I have a beautiful collection of old art prints and I manage, with my husband and my best friend who is a banker, my financial investments in order to pass them down to my children.

I have deliberately shortened these two portraits a little in order to simplify them, because the main thing was that you should understand the process of making your own portrait. Feel free to be more precise and to write down more details. It is necessary that you describe yourself well in all your aspects, mentioning what *is* important what might *seem* important to you— both positive and negative aspects, as I said before.

Keep this document in a safe place, as we will need it later.

To sum up :

☑ We are going to write our balance sheet on a piece of paper.

☑ We begin by writing down everything we are and every-thing that constitutes our existence, element by element: physical, mental, character, occupations, relationships, work, etc.

☑ We link these elements together to write a half-page to one-page text that will be our portrait.

☑ This is a very powerful psychological exercise.

CHAPTER 15
SETTING A GOAL

*"Man needs a goal; not having one is
to be half-dead"*
Pierre-Claude-Victor Boiste

When I talk to people and the conversation allows it, I find it very informative to ask them what their goal in life is. Not everyone has one, and few have a clear plan.

Those who truly have definite goal manage to answer my question without thinking specifically. Their goals are many and varied, but their determination is obvious. Whether they want to move to another country, double their income, start a school, marry a Miss world or Mr. Universe contestant, or drive a Rolls-Royce, they know what they want.

Those who do not have a goal do not respond in the same way. First, they think. Then they are vaguer, and their sentences look something like: "A goal? Uh... Ah... Well... Yes, of course, to be happy, for my children to succeed, to be healthy," etc. These generalities, which we all desire, have nothing to do with a specific goal.

A goal should be as specific and precise as possible.

These people do not ask themselves the question, or rather, no longer ask themselves the question; they stopped doing so a long time ago. It is certain that in their youth they had dreams, like all children, but they have since abandoned them.

This is not their fault. The society in which we live does not teach us this kind of thing, and many people get discouraged from dreaming at all.

Man is not made to live without a goal. Many who were at one-point battling depression began to feel their symptoms alleviate the moment they found a goal. The existence of those who have a goal is much fuller than that of those who do not. Performing daily tasks one after the other by adapting to circumstances is not a goal. It is merely surviving.

Can we imagine a boat or plane leaving the port or the airport without any roadmap, without any precise timetable, route, or destination?

Without an objective, the human being will also be like a boat drifting on the waves.

A goal will give you motivation, discipline and action.

The recipe for self-confidence, which is the object of this program, consists mainly of two ingredients: a favorable attitude and a clear goal. This attitude and goal will magically attract favorable circumstances.

Achieving one's goal is not the only advantage of having *set* one. A worthy goal will also allow us to reap many benefits along the way as we move towards its realization.

Let's take a closer look at this by taking an example. The following case is of course extreme, but the *modus operandi* is the same:

In 1995, Guy Delage was the first to swim across the Atlantic. It took him fifty-five days, swimming eight hours a day and drifting on his buoy the rest of the time. He will later confess to having gained more satisfaction *during* his crossing than at the finish once his feat was achieved.

We reap the benefits of a goal in every moment that progress towards its achievement, beginning the minute we set it.

The point of setting a goal is not to *achieve* something, but to *evolve*. This goal must be new to us, and we must not know how to reach it. It must seem out of reach.

You will only know how to succeed once you have succeeded, that is where the secret lies. This is how you can acquire new know-how. The problem is that very often we think backwards.

Setting a goal today and knowing how to reach it is of no interest. We must have new neurons working; it's the price of evolution. We must go into the unknown, make new experiences, and "stretch" ourselves to the maximum so that our approach is useful for something.

This goal must respond to a deep desire that really excites us.

A mistake we make too often— not to say every day— is to limit ourselves, effectively extinguishing our motivation.

We have already learned the power of emotion to impact our minds, so our goal must really come from the heart— or the gut, as they say. We must choose what we really want deep down inside.

There is no reason to limit our choices to what we *believe* we can achieve. Only a faulty self-image can lead us to accept this kind of compromise.

So why shouldn't *we* achieve *our* dreams when so many others do? We have before us enough examples of beautiful achievements, whether they are made by famous people or in our circle of friends. The secret of these achievements is quite simple: there was an initial goal, a vision, and a burning desire to achieve it.

Learning a new language can be an excellent goal and a remarkable evolutionary factor. Your brain is just waiting for this kind of challenge. Unless, of course, you learned French or Spanish last year, in which case learning a new language will not be a worthwhile goal since you already know how to do it.

Wanting to buy a car when you can afford it is also not a worthy goal, because there is no challenge. On the other hand, if you have never owned a car and you don't have enough money, that changes everything. This is a great goal because we will have to get out of our "comfort zone," find an honest solution, and act to achieve the desired result.

Do you want to learn to play a musical instrument? Do you have a professional or family goal? A trip to take? Something to buy or give as a gift? The possibilities are endless.

Here is a list of goals that have been selected by several people. They are all valid, if they meet the stated conditions:

- Buy an apartment, a house, or a car
- Open a school.
- Move to another country.
- Grow a business.
- Take a trip.
- Achieve a high level of sporting performance.
- Change jobs.
- Help someone else achieve something.
- Double or multiply one's income.
- Become an actor or a singer.
- Write a book.
- Etc.

If your goal is not immediately obvious, it is still best to use a sheet of paper. Using your imagination— like making a shopping list— make a list of anything you would like to do or have. The principle is always the same. Sitting with a pen in your hand in front of a sheet of paper can answer many questions.

When this list is established, rank the different items in order of priority. The one at the top will be your goal, it's as simple as that.

Now that you have a goal, write it down and write a sentence in the present tense, as if you have already reached your goal. Be specific and don't hesitate to add a few details that may reinforce your intent.

Also write in the introduction:

"I am happy and grateful now"

We will come back to this way of proceeding when we discuss the notion of "present time".

For example, if you have decided to set up a real estate agency, write something like:

"I am happy and grateful now to have set up my real estate agency, which allows me to help many people find the homes they are looking for"

It is this kind of internal dialogue that we will now learn to develop and maintain.

Believe me, it will prove to be more productive than spending your time worrying. The more you have these kinds of thoughts in your mind, the more your confidence will grow. Keep your goal in mind, and your brain will automatically start looking for solutions on its own.

Put this sentence aside with your personal balance sheet, we will need it in the following chapters to integrate it into your work.

To sum up :

- ☑ We are going to set ourselves a main goal.
- ☑ It must be a dream, a very deep desire. It must excite us.
- ☑ It must be new, and we must not know today how we will reach it.
- ☑ The real objective of the goal is to make us grow.

CHAPTER 16
WRITING YOUR SELF-PORTRAIT

"As far as the future is concerned, it's
all about making it possible"
Antoine de Saint-Exupéry

Now let's get down to business: we are going to write our final portrait, which we will call "My Self-portrait". It is thanks to this practice and the way we will work on it that we will succeed in gradually modifying our *self-image*.

Recall the assessment previously written in Chapter 14 ("Balance sheet") as it will serve as a basis for our work.

The difference this time is that you are going to compose the portrait of the person you are going to become, or, to be more precise, the portrait of the person you really are, deep down inside yourself; this character that corresponds to your tastes and desires, and that was not created according to circumstances or outside elements. On the contrary, this character was created according to your balance sheet.

To do this, take the same sentences and rework them, emphasizing what you already like about yourself, and changing what you perceive to be flaws.

In doing so, you will again focus more specifically on the aspects that concern you.

It may be new to you but do it; this method is very effective.

In this portrait, include as an introduction, the sentence describing the goal you wrote in Chapter 15 ("Setting a Goal").

This portrait must be written in the *present* tense too. Future tense does not convey the same message to the unconscious as present tense. Thinking, "I'm going to be happy," does not bring the same emotions as, "I'm happy," does.

The other reason seems obvious. To say, "I'm *going* to be happy," is to say that you are not happy today. In the mind of the person who wants to achieve it, a goal must be in the present.

Of course, this is the first step. It is not enough to think and assert one's desires as already realized. It is necessary to be moved by them, to feel them deeply, vividly, and to adapt one's inner dialogue. It is only then that our actions are impacted by our desires and that they naturally lead us towards our goals.

As you write your self-portrait, mark a blank line after each sentence to make your statements stand out and let the text breathe.

Be careful not to use negative phrasing: write, "I meet people easily," rather than, "I have no trouble meeting people".

Use phrases that describe positive and strong emotions, such as, "I am happy," "I have the pleasure of," "I am proud of," etc.

This text will describe what you want to be; a kind of ideal to which you aspire and which you will come closer to each time you work on it.

Use your imagination in your new self-portrait. Don't be afraid to push the limits as far as your desires take you. It's very important; it's your life. It's *your* story we're talking about, not someone else's. *You're* the main character, so think big. Under no circumstances would you want to settle for a supporting role. You don't need to go so far as to declare yourself the physical-intellectual mix of George Clooney and Albert Einstein or Megan Fox and Marie Curie, with the financial latitude of Jeff Bezos! But you must think big.

Children put up posters of their idols in their rooms, and adults put their own portraits, and they both have an effect.

It is now a matter of thinking in these terms: you are the hero of your existence. Don't limit yourself. If you limit yourself even in your imagination and in your desires, what can you expect in your daily life?

You will learn to stay in tune with where you are going, not where you are. You are going to present yourself to the world as the person you are becoming in the same way that when you go to a party, you dress for the event to come and not for the moment.

If you think that "you shouldn't exaggerate," that you should "keep a sense of reality," and if you feel a form of discomfort, you can be sure that the image of your current self has just taken over to slow you down and limit you. Don't take this self-sabotage as reason; it is not.

We know that the level of your ego of today watches and stands guard, to prevent you from changing, because it is afraid of disappearing. It doesn't want to fade away, even in favor of a more evolved state. It unmasks itself by betraying, once again, your interests. The complexity of the unconscious is endless.

We have already said it: mysticism is not to think that we can control our lives ourselves, but to believe that it would be controlled by mysterious external forces.

Describe yourself the way you really want to be by changing your perception. However, it's obvious that if you're 5'10", you can't write, "I'm 6'10"— in this case, make sentences such as, "My 5'10" height is ideal," or, "I'm the perfect height"— since your goal now is to increase your self-satisfaction.

Nature does things well, and it is also very unlikely that you will have the desire to aim for a goal that you know can't achieve. The fact that you desire something should carry with it the possibility of obtaining it.

Let us replace in our minds the expression, "not to take one's desires for realities," with, "We must take our desires for possibilities".

Every aspect of your existence will be addressed again in this self-portrait:

- Appearance.
- Physical condition, hygiene.
- Personality, character, mental.
- Behavior.
- Relationship to others.
- Job.
- Finances.
- Activities, occupations, and hobbies.

The easiest way to do this work and write your new portrait is, as we saw above, to take each sentence of your assessment, one after the other, and modify them according to my instructions.

Do not hesitate to remove statements that you no longer feel are necessary, or to add others (even if they have nothing to do with the previous text), because our perception changes every day.

You are already evolving while doing this work, and it is likely that many new ideas come to you every day. Think about orienting your self-portrait according to your needs.

Insist on what is worth working on. If you have just won the Wimbledon tournament, there is no need to dwell on your level of tennis, everything is already in order.

You can write long sentences with descriptions or multiple elements, but there should only be one theme or topic per sentence.

Leave a space between each sentence.

This crucial exercise will be carried out scrupulously, giving maximum thought to the choice of each word. Each statement must be precise and free of vague turns or subjective elements. In other words, favor, "I run and swim once a week," to, "I regularly practice several sports".

It is certain that this work will take you several days, perhaps even weeks, if you wish to establish a satisfactory self-portrait. This is not a problem, it's part of the job, and your mind is already in motion.

You will find that you will continue to change your portrait day after day while working on it in small touches; changing a sentence here, another one there, a word a little further on. This text will evolve in a fluid way, at the rhythm of your own evolution.

As you perform this exercise, you will experience a deep cleansing feeling, like a good mental shower.

You will understand perfectly how to proceed by going back to the examples of Franck and Caroline whom we met in chapter 14 ("Balanced sheet"), and whose new self-portraits are presented in the next chapter.

You will find in these stories, the present tense, the spaces between sentences, the emphasis on qualities, revised defects, positive sensations, etc.

Finally, don't hesitate to compose sentences that involve you and concern the major themes evoked in the first theoretical part of this book. Here are some of them as a reminder:

- The importance of setting a goal to evolve.
- The quality of our thoughts.
- The causes (thoughts) versus consequences (actions).
- The choice of people and places we frequent.
- The choice of our occupations.
- Thinking from the sensation of our *realized* desires, rather than thinking about our desires.
- The enormous capacities of the human being; it's all a question of trust and intention.
- The notions of interior and exterior, and not to weaken in the face of circumstances.

- The importance of repetition; working and studying daily.
- Repetition to "print" in the unconscious.
- The feeling of gratitude.
- The feeling of responsibility in our attitude.
- The importance of innovating and constantly moving out of our comfort zone.
- Fear (in all its forms) is defeated by knowledge.

To sum up :

- ☑ We are going to write our self-portrait which will form the basis of our work.
- ☑ The self-portrait is the portrait of the person we have decided to be.
- ☑ The choice of each word is crucial, and the writing of the self-portrait will take at least several days.
- ☑ We are the protagonist of this portrait.
- ☑ We write it in the present tense, spacing out the sentences and addressing a single theme in each one.
- ☑ This self-portrait will always be on the move and we will modify and adapt it as we evolve.

CHAPTER 17
EXAMPLES OF SELF-PORTRAITS

"He who does not have an ideal does not risk reaching it"

Sun Tse

New self-portrait of Franck.

I have added comments after each sentence to help you establish yours.

You will notice that this story is much more complete and elaborate than the portrait of his balance sheet. You will do the same.

> "I am happy and grateful now, in 2019, to have increased my salary and to earn $6,000 each month by working consistently and regularly in the city of X".

The self-portrait begins with the goal and the words, "I am happy and grateful now". Franck's goal is to increase his salary this year to 6,000 dollars per month. It is important to be precise in setting an exact amount; Statements such as "a lot," "largely," "very," etc. mean nothing in a self-portrait. In addition, Frank has also decided to not change jobs on a regular basis as he used to before.

My name is Franck X, I'm 5'9" tall with short, brown hair.

and I have a pleasant face.

This is a statement that develops confidence, to be used without moderation.

I am healthy, very fit, and my body is working wonderfully.

Here, Franck had first written, "I am in great shape, because I am never sick," I had him rephrase the sentence to eliminate the negative connotation.

I appreciate when people regularly compliment me on my physique.

Don't be afraid to use these kinds of statements, especially for those whose inner monologue has been at the opposite end of the spectrum for years. It is better to repeat to yourself that you like it than the other way around. As we have seen, it is good to incorporate emotional formulas such as "I am happy" or "I appreciate".

I dress elegantly and stylishly, and I take a lot of care in choosing my outfits.

Here, Frank works on his deep image by expressing another of his goals, since his outfits are often neglected.

I regularly practice many sports in clubs, especially tennis, football and volleyball.

Franck had written, "I am very athletic". I made him add some details. These are very important, as we will see later when we learn how to work on it.

I eat a healthy diet and I am happy to see my figure improve day by day.

This is not a reality today and that is the purpose of the self-portrait. Franck is going to influence his unconscious by working regularly on this sentence; A surefire way to maintain his motivation and to trigger certain mechanisms.

I am curious about everything and I like to cultivate myself by reading every day and getting informed in different ways.

I am fluent in four languages, thanks to my excellent memory and my appetite for learning languages.

Here, Franck puts two elements in one sentence: he is both a polyglot and has a good memory. Combining several elements is beneficial when the themes are close and coherent, because the self-portrait should not be too long. However, it is not beneficial to include sentences like, "I speak four languages, I am very fit, and I am very proud of my magnificent stamp collection".

My language abilities allow me to have very diverse contacts during my many trips.

I am joyful and dynamic, so I am an enterprising person and I am grateful for my existence.

Here again, we find four elements: joy, dynamism, extroversion, and gratitude mixed together, but it is coherent. As in many other statements, Franck insists on his qualities and he takes advantage of this to feel gratitude.

> I feel compassion for myself as well as for others. I love myself and I love people.

One of his challenges is to become more respectful of those around him.

> It is with this enthusiasm that I meet many people every day, and I love forming these new relationships.

Here, Franck is revising his slightly gruff side.

> I talk to all kinds of people, and I listen carefully when they talk to me. I am very kind and respectful to everyone.

Here, Franck reviews his difficulty in accepting people whom he defines as "stuck". Franck has written several sentences about his relational characteristics. I pointed this out to him, and he indicated that he really wanted to emphasize this aspect of his personality that is sometimes a bit brittle.

> I am very friendly with everyone but remain very selective about the people I regularly interact with.

He is right, one does not prevent the other.

> I am single and I have a strong aptitude for partying, due to my cheerful character.

I am appreciated by those around me for my frankness and enthusiasm.

I'm deepening my close relationships to build stronger bonds.

Franck has many acquaintances and few close friends. He is sometimes criticized for being superficial.

I work in the restaurant business, in the city of X. I manage my business by focusing on my current position, and in order to enhance my skills and income.

Another of Franck's "challenges", remember.

I love to cook, which also allows me to help the chef when necessary.

Yet another area of interest. Franck is curious and enthusiastic.

This also allows me the joy of building customer loyalty by bringing them pleasure.

Congratulations to Franck, he understood everything: pleasant sensations and mutual benefits.

I take flying lessons every day off, flying an airplane has been my dream since I was a child.

In fact, it was a secondary project, but Franck could also have made it his primary goal. I recommended that he give himself three evenings to research this via the internet, then to go and register and make a first payment in a club within the following ten days.

Making quick decisions and executing them immediately is a guarantee of success and happiness.

> Every day relaxed and focused, I spend 20-30 minutes working on my self-portrait.

Either 10-15 minutes in the morning when waking up, and then again in the evening before going to sleep.

The portrait of Franck is of course not complete here, but I think you have understood how to do it.

There are no rules, but experience has taught me that a complete self-portrait usually contains about thirty to forty sentences. Remember to address all the themes in your life, preferably in the following order:

- Aspect, appearance.
- Physical condition, hygiene.
- Character, mind and behavior.
- Relationship.
- Work and finance.
- Occupations, distractions, and leisure activities.

With about five to six well-considered and thoughtfully worded statements per main theme, you'll be there. Your self-portrait will be complete enough without being too long to work on it for a few minutes every day without getting discouraged.

New self-portrait of Caroline

Here is the second example of Caroline's self-portrait. It is obviously written according to the same rules, and should, along with Franck's, help you write yours.

> "I am happy and grateful now to start my own photography company by March, and to train young people and promote this wonderful passion"

For her goal, Caroline gives herself three months.

Note that this sentence is obviously only a summary of her goal. Caroline also drew up a detailed plan that she wrote, marking the successive stages of her project in a very precise manner (finding partners, establishing a business plan, approaching banks, raising funds, legally constituting her company, etc.)

She will follow this roadmap which includes deadlines.

> My name is Caroline Y, I am 5.7 feet.

Always, after goal statement of course, start with an introductory sentence.

> I am enthusiastic and I am someone who loves my life.

One of the challenges of this process is to open up and become a little more extroverted and less cautious.

> The features of my face are pleasant and graceful, and I am happy to be pretty.

Statements such as these are extremely powerful in gradually changing one's perception. Caroline found it very difficult to write such a sentence. She had difficulty seeing herself as pretty, and she limited herself considerably in this area.

> I am slim and I enjoy paying attention to my outfit, which I would describe as quite classic, and in which I feel good.

Some people reproach her for her style, finding it "bland". Here, Caroline assumes her style and asserts it.

> I attach great importance to cleanliness. Therefore, I am a very neat person.

> I am married to Eric who protects me, in a harmonious relationship where we blossom mutually.

> We have two beautiful children, Karen and Brian, and the four of us spend a lot of time together as a family. We organize many games together at home, and outings on weekends.

Family values are very important to Caroline, and a key factor in her development.

> I am an honest and sincere person, and I take great pride in my morality.

Pride is a powerful stimulant; it is a strong emotion.

> Every day, people know they can count on me and I recognize that I am very much appreciated for that.

Caroline cultivates and maintains her qualities, in addition to reviewing her weak points.

> I have very good friends that I like to go out with, and thanks to my open attitude, I regularly grow this circle of friends.

Caroline has never had a problem in close relationships with her current friends, but she wants more.

> When I meet new people, I am very attentive and have a pleasant conversation with them. They are also happy to have this new contact with me.

Caroline comes back to it. She wants to be less shy and more outgoing towards others; this is one of her main challenges. Moreover, she has always been naturally interested in others.

> I go to the gym twice a week to exercise and for yoga classes.

Caroline maintains her motivation and discipline; they are rituals for her.

> I watch what I eat. I eat mostly fruits and vegetables, and I'm happy to have a flat stomach.
>
> This lifestyle and these practices bring me great balance and allow me to manage my health day after day. This allows me and my husband to travel more and more.

We know that Caroline's health is a concern. The doctor caring for her strongly encourages her to take charge of the triptych of exercise, nutrition, and sleep. It was he who advised her to take yoga classes, and now she can go on vacations more often with her husband.

> I have always been passionate about art in all its forms and I love to develop my tastes and increase my knowledge, especially in the field of photography.

A passion is like a goal; it is a guarantee of happiness.

> I have made my passion my profession. I am a photographer, and I am happy to see commissions and contracts pouring in in large numbers.

Here again, Caroline doesn't need to force her talent.

> This is surely also since I am extremely meticulous and well-organized, and that I do not hesitate to spend hours improving the photos I provide for my clients.

> This success that I achieve by indulging in my passion allows me to contribute to the comfort of my family. This ability brings me a lot of happiness.

The power of emotions and strong feelings.

> I invested, with the help of my bank, in a country house 60 kilometers from the city to visit with my family on weekends. I also help many people by donating to charities.

Always mutual benefit: the culmination of success.

> I collect fine art prints, especially from the 1930s; it is both a hobby for me and a financial investment.

> With my husband and with the help of my best friend who works in a bank, we each put 15% of our salary aside for our children's futures.

No doubt that Caroline, with so many qualities, will go even further. She became aware of all these advantages when she wrote her self-portrait, and this gave her a lot of confidence.

Here again, this self-portrait has been shortened, it contains about ten sentences more.

To sum up :

☑ We write our self-portrait by describing ourselves and all aspects of our existence.

☑ We affirm our strengths and qualities.

☑ We focus on the points we want to work on— sometimes using several sentences about our challenges— and revise our perception and vocabulary.

☑ Thirty to forty sentences are enough to establish a self-portrait.

☑ We will work every day and in a very specific way on this self-portrait.

CHAPTER 18
WORKING ON YOUR SELF-PORTRAIT

"Become what you are"
Friedrich Nietzsche

By thinking seriously and through methodical work, you have just built, in full awareness, your new portrait. You have developed it according to your real personality, and it contrasts the old one which developed through random circumstances and events.

This work has allowed you to clarify things by becoming more conscious, and to regain control by giving more of yourself to the person you really are.

You can record your self-portrait— which I recommend— but you can also work from the paper version or from the page on your computer (explanations are given at the end of this chapter).

You will now work daily on this self-portrait, so that this new image replaces the old one. This work will of course be done progressively, according to the rhythm of your work sessions, a bit like two glasses placed one next to the other. Imagine that you gradually remove the liquid from one glass in order to fill the second one. The human brain needs repetition and time to accept any new idea. Your unconscious will gradually see the new model take precedence over the old one, until one day it is completely replaced.

Soon, when you think of yourself, the image that will come to mind will be that of your self-portrait.

When Galileo confirmed after Copernicus that the Earth was not the center of the universe, he revealed this to the whole world. Initially, no one believed him, and he was even imprisoned for professing such an idea, but little by little, people admitted the validity of this idea and finally made it a certainty.

You will also see a synergistic effect, since this regular work will lead to new behaviors in you that will, in turn, accelerate this replacement process. It is the snowball that picks up speed as it descends a slope due to the progressive increase in its weight.

Progress will be significant in a short time and this dynamic will keep you motivated and help you persevere.

However, you will have to work on a regular basis; every day. Make it a ritual; it is imperative if you want this evolution to be constant. Don't forget that the old image was built up over many years! Change cannot happen overnight, especially since we are aiming for definitive progress.

To do this, one must tackle not the consequences, but the causes, by modifying one's system of thought.

One of the two key words in this case is *repetition*, which is one of the gateways leading to the unconscious.

Our beliefs and attitudes have been imprinted deep within us by the relentless repetition of unconscious thoughts, and the only way to change them is to use the same process. Therefore, the work must be done daily, and this is how the content of the unconscious will change.

Hoping to permanently change our old image in another way is unfortunately no more conceivable than to immediately change bad form in a sport, for example. If your golf swing is not perfect enough, you will have to repeat the new gesture correctly dozens and dozens of times before it becomes the default motion.

The other gateway to the unconscious is *mental imagery*. We can also use the terms *visualization or motor imagery*.

Mental imagery or visualization

When we previously mentioned the unconscious, we noted that it did not make the distinction between an imagined situation and a situation really lived; this is a primordial element that we will take advantage of.

Dreams allow us to understand this phenomenon. When we sleep and dream about a situation, we live it completely and feel all the emotions attached to it. This imaginary mental creation is for us, a reality, and the impact is the same as what we experience when we are awake.

It is also easy to *feel* a state instantly through imagination; if we think of a happy event, we will be happy; if we think of a sad event, we will be sad.

Mental imagery consists of mentally experiencing a situation and, with the help of the imagination, making it as real and alive as possible.

In this case, let's close our eyes and imagine ourselves as being and acting according to our desires; succeeding in every task we undertake.

We need to feel— physically and emotionally— our mental creation so that all elements of reality are recreated. The mind needs concrete details, striking images, and sensations. We must experience with all our senses (sounds, physical sensations, tastes, smells, and of course, visions etc.) in order to achieve maximum efficiency. Physical sensations and emotions are the ingredients that differentiate mental imagery from simple affirmations and assertions.

The goal is not to *recite* our self-portrait, but to *live* it. "The art of living is to sustain the feeling of fulfilled desire," said Neville Goddard.

You need to experiment yourself to see which method works best for you. As you experiment, this will become more and more effective, and you will learn a lot about how you work.

In 90% of cases, people find it more profitable to see themselves performing the actions from the inside (doing the actions themselves), rather than from the outside (like watching themselves in a movie projected on a screen).

If we visualize ourselves driving a car, we are sitting in the driver's seat; we see our arms, the steering wheel we grasp, the dashboard, and we feel all the sensations of driving. We see the road in front of us, the scenery, the other vehicles, the sky, the sun, the signs. We feel the seat under our buttocks and the gas pedal and brake under our feet. We feel in our hands, the contact of the steering wheel and the gear lever when we manipulate it. We feel if they are hard, soft, rough, hot, or cold. We hear the sounds of the car, the engine, the transmission, the wheels on the road, and the wind. We smell leather, maybe gasoline, or exhaust. We are perfectly at ease and we perform all these movements in the best possible way.

This is the description of a well-executed visualization. Don't be frustrated if you don't reach such a level of accuracy. Any visualization exercise is effective, and we just must try to do our best, knowing that, with practice, we will improve.

Some other examples of visualizations

If we give a speech in front of a large public, we see ourselves executing it perfectly, without trembling, without searching for our words, and we notice that the crowd listens to us with great attention, before giving ourselves over to a thunderous applause when we have finished.

When we make a sale, we visualize all the details; our arrival at the appointment, the quality of our prospective client's welcome and interview, our convincing answers to questions or objections, the acceptance of our contract, the warmth of our client's handshake, his joy at the signing, and his grateful smile when we part.

Last example: if a person is not satisfied with his gait— which he finds heavy and awkward— he will see himself evolve with lightness and elegance, always in a very precise way, integrating all the corresponding sensations, without forgetting the pleasure of feeling agile.

If you want to give it a try, imagine yourself biting into a lemon, and see if you can feel the acidity of the fruit.

It is really necessary to abound in detail to impact the unconscious. It is only at this price that the visualized event has the value of reality.

By adding 100% optimism and positivity without any complexes— as we did when we wrote our self-portrait— we make this process particularly effective in increasing our confidence.

What we want to see concretely realized is first imagined in the brain.

If by chance this procedure is new to you, you should know that it has been practiced by countless people around the world since the dawn of time. In all religions, large and small, you will find many references to visualization.

Aristotle said, "The thinking faculty thinks its forms in mental images".

Galileo, Newton, Copernicus, and Einstein— to name a few— were known to practice visualization.

Napoleon to erase obstacles from his brain. He himself said, "I see only my objective; the obstacle must disappear".

Nikola Tesla would dream for hours— in a state of wakefulness— about his future inventions.

Thomas Edison saw himself as the person who would illuminate the world and he kept that vision in his mind constantly.

Lincoln and Churchill— like so many other politicians, — practiced their speeches in their imaginations before returning to their audiences.

Graham Hill— the 1976 Formula One World Champion— would sit in his car at a standstill before each race, close his eyes and visualize his entire route, with all the details of the circuits he knew by heart.

Tiger Woods makes the perfect swing in his head before stepping onto the green.

Dr. Vandell of New York conducted experiments on archers in the 1960s, having them shoot imaginative arrows into targets each day for an hour. He stated that the progress made was equivalent to that achieved by actual training.

Research Quarterly magazine cites a twenty-day basketball experiment. A first group of students practiced shooting the balls into the basket every day. A second group did it through visualization. The third group did not practice at all. The first group improved their scores by 24%, and the second group by 23%, while the level of the last group remained unchanged.

In April 1955, *Reader's Digest* published an article by Joseph Phillips that recounts how Alexander Alekhine— a chess player— defeated, to the amazement of all, José Raúl Capablanca— a player with a much higher rating. Alekhine had retired to the countryside, abstained from tobacco and alcohol for three months, and played chess in his imagination, concentrating more and more on the game.

In his book, *Secrets of Closing Sales*, Charles B. Roth talks about the same experience with a team of sales representatives in Detroit. They mentally trained for three months, using the principles of imagery to make sales. They improved 100% and doubled their sales. The experience was replicated in New York City, where the salespeople improved by 150%. They informed another group of salespeople from a New York company of their results which motivated them, and they, in turn, conducted a new experiment; this time the result was an increase of 400%!

Artur Schnabel— a world-renowned pianist known for his unique interpretations of Schubert's repertoire (which is not the easiest)— said he practiced mostly in his head, as he hated to do it the traditional way.

I could go on giving you examples for hundreds of pages; the list is endless. Whatever their discipline, all the best have practiced this technique.

Mental imagery combined with your self-portrait will therefore prove to be a wonderful tool. As I said before, it is a true *recipe for success*.

For the effects of the visualization to be optimal, you need to be very relaxed. Its effectiveness will be all the greater the more your brain rhythm is in alpha frequency; this is the rhythm it is in when you wake up, or just before falling asleep.

You've figured out the best times to do this activity, but you can also reach this state (the alpha frequency) at any time of day if you are calm, or if you relax for five minutes.

If possible, try to stay in the right frame of mind throughout the day. Be in harmony with your new knowledge. Your desires and your projects can be seen as two people; they have to agree to be able to move together in the same direction.

Working on your self-portrait will help you evolve considerably. You can be sure of this and expect the benefits of confidence while being fully relaxed. The results will present themselves to you as surely as a dish ordered in a restaurant.

Do not hesitate, as already mentioned, to improve your self-portrait regularly (and to re-record it) by changing words, phrases, or themes as you go along. This double evolution— yours and your self-portrait's— will prove to be very motivating and dynamic.

Viewing your self-portrait will take about 10 to 15 minutes each session.

You will of course do it all at once, without interruption, isolating yourself from any distractions and remaining fully concentrated throughout the session.

Doing this work once a day is already effective, but I recommend doing it twice (morning and evening, for example) especially in the early stages.

How to do it?

Make sure you are relaxed, comfortably settled down, and revisit your self-portrait.

Read each sentence, then pause with your eyes closed and use mental imagery for 10 to 20 seconds.

You can also listen to your self-portrait with your eyes closed if you have recorded it, in which case you will have inserted fifteen-second silence periods after each sentence to give you time to visualize your affirmations.

How to record your self-portrait?

You can make this recording directly on your cell phone or on your computer; these devices all now have recording capabilities.

If you want to make a high-quality recording (without background noise) and then want to manipulate it in different ways, there are many software programs that offer very convenient, accessible and free functions on the internet; "**Audacity**" among many others for example. Don't worry if you're not a geek— as I am— they are very easy-to-use tool. With them, you can easily create quality recordings and improve or modify them later, without having to start all over again.

You will be able to add silence between sentences, adjust the volume, eliminate white noise, remove, add or move sentences without having to start your recording from the beginning. No doubt there are many other features that I don't know about that will allow you to go much further to increase the quality of your recordings. But that's not the point.

IT'S UP TO YOU!

You now have in your hands, a tool that will take you very far. It's now up to you.

Working on your self-portrait every day is the best method I know of to improve your *self-image* and change your old limiting beliefs about yourself.

Every day, you will become more efficient in your actions and your progress towards your goals.

I can only wish you a safe journey in the wonderful, personal adventure that lies ahead of you.

Made in the USA
Monee, IL
04 September 2023

42115264R00109